Politics or Quality?

Nisbet Media Ltd
29 Mellstock Avenue
Dorchester
Dorset DT1 2BG
email: books@nisbetmedia.co.uk

First Publ.ished 2006
Designed by Julian Slade
Typeset in Warnock Pro

ISBN 0-9553000-0-2
ISBN 978-0-9553000-0-4

Published by Nisbet Media Ltd
© Dave Gaster

Printed in England

Politics or Quality?

A view of service delivery in Local Government since 1980

DAVE GASTER

Nisbet media

CONTENTS

Introduction

This book focuses on the achievement of *quality* in services mainly within local government, addressing the impacts of government, with a number of case studies and examples of how *Best Value* and *Continuous Improvement* can really be addressed. Against this there is the paradox of an increasing level of legislation and re-interpretation by the government plus a reducing interest in local government from the electorate.

The nature of business management and government in Britain has, over the last twenty five years, been more and more focussed on short-termism. Big businesses must focus on the stock exchange, where even growth of income and margin can cause stocks to lose value, and suspicions of suspicions can cause the whole market to collapse.

The national government is run in a series of four to five year sprints, with promises made, and often forgotten and a culture of blame and recrimination permeating the top management, seeking to meddle in everyone's affairs. The speed of change is such that even before ideas are fine tuned they can be subject to another change.

Then there are Counties, Districts, Towns, Parishes, Unitaries, and regional layers of local government, overlaid and intertwined with a plethora of agencies. Even here new entities are being considered, the new spirit of government is heading in two, apparently diametrically opposed directions. The pursuit of regional government appears to be happening by stealth giving greater powers to centres of excellence. Then there is the need to get closer to communities with a focus on neighbourhoods. This could lead to the creation of parishes in authorities without them, or some degree of devolution to unelected bodies to spend monies locally with a degree of enforcement potential.

More than 90 per cent of local government functions are a legal requirement:

• Provide education services from the age of three to ninety three
• Have a social care responsibility
• Provide, support, maintain, and develop transport, and roads.
• Collect and dispose of refuse, with ever increasing mandates to divert materials away from landfill.
• Ensure sustainable planning for regions, areas, towns and individuals

Local government used to do more, but services have been stripped away, or privatised over a long period:

• Provision of gas and electricity
• Water provision and waste water treatment
• Housing provision - rapidly becoming impossible solely inside local government.

Most of this is handcuffed by legislation, BVPI's, best practice etc, with a funding regime that makes authorities jump through hoops to qualify for a little more cash. Since the poll tax, the percentage of spend that comes from the central government is greater than ever, and thus councils have a reducing capability for local governance, as they have less say on what they may do, and less control on how they can fund it.

The distribution of funding from the centre is highly political, and could get worse. There is also a proliferation of quangos which generally consists of unelected, non-democratic boards, distributing cash out in a number of ways. Then there are PFIs, lottery money, Neighbourhood Renewal Funds... and a huge list of ways to get more cash. Inner city poverty is currently understood by central government and is therefore funded, but is rural poverty either understood or funded?

Strangely the electorate is not very concerned about local elections, particularly as even small councils still generally have the same political parties standing as for national elections. Central government determine over 90% of what happens locally, so why should local politicians make any difference?

Lastly, we look at who does this work. Prior to 1980, local government had a freedom of choice as to whether it did work directly, or if it contracted it out to others. This caused the start of Compulsory Competitive Tendering, (CCT) initially via the Local government Planning and Land Act 1980, and later via the Local Government Act 1988.

The first Act was introduced at the start of a long Conservative administration which is generally held up as typical of Conservatives forcing work out to the Private sector. Most people fail to recall that this Act was introduced as a Bill in 1979 by the Labour Party, as they wanted to prove that direct works contracts within local government were competitive.

This affected only a relatively narrow band of employment within local government, enabling almost a two tier division, those who had to comply with it, and those who didn't.

The introduction of CCT led directly to the establishment of Direct Labour Organisations (DLOs) covering; Highway Maintenance, Housing Maintenance, Sewers, and Public Lighting mainly. It also started slowly, a form of bedding in period. Targets were set for when work had to be won, how much, and the need to make profits (Rate of return on capital employed). ROCE was an interesting concept based on SSAP16 (this is basically an Accountants tool for measuring how good a business is doing when working in extreme inflationary times such as in the mid 70's)

SSAP 16 was developed for the private sector, and then effectively never used, as rampant inflation has, so far, not returned to this country. What was required was for a DLO to make at least 5% return on capital employed, thus if you had £1,000,000 worth of equipment within the contract, you had to make £50,000 worth of profit. The game became one of reducing capital via leasing, so you had no assets, thus needed no minimum profit level.

As time went on the ratio of work done after competition increased, and DLOs generally either got bigger, or went out of existence, depending on success.

While this had its positive effects, and that small proportion of affected services improved their commercial capabilities, much of the core of local government was largely unaffected. Some councils found this first phase difficult or impossible to live with, and as a result decided, or were forced to, reduce or pull out of the competitive arena.

Those who lived successfully with it found a number of loop-holes in the legislation and therefore exploited the options presenting themselves. We were entering a new era of the entrepreneur within local government. This created internal pressures as many services were not included in these new ways of working and this brought new frictions.

One of the most frequent complaints from inside DLOs was that the government was not keeping a level playing field. That they always made it harder to succeed than win.

This also impacted on the support services such as finance, personnel and administration. The financial aspects of CCT required services to be purchased for a price, with an internal market driven by SLAs. (Service Level Agreements). Thus the contracting areas fought hard to get more service for less cost, and that, more than anything else, caused trouble.

In 1988 the Local Government Act came into being, causing virtually all blue collar services to need to be tendered, and these would have Direct Service Organisations (DSOs) set up to do the work. This covered areas like: refuse, street cleansing, grounds maintenance, school meals and leisure services all of which then needed to be competed for.

This was a whole new ball game, as highway maintenance had historically always had contracts, and contractors to do some of the work, but refuse collection just happened, didn't it? So complete new professional areas had to grow; people who could write contracts, and enforce them for the public benefit and contractors who could tender for that work, do the job, and make it pay.

We still had government holding legislation and the purse strings, so why not change the rules so that housing associations could buy council houses, and through differing powers to re-invest money and be in a better position to run the housing stock. Let's also force councils to sell the best properties under the right to buy, at less than market value, and while they keep the worst ones, not let them use the capital receipts to create new homes.

Other new legislation caused layer upon layer of new issues to be resolved. As DLOs and DSOs worked out how to get less people to do more work, bonus schemes became incentivators to achieve greater volumes of work. The old practices of excessive sickness rates were often eradicated by effectively having attendance bonuses. It was then a financial burden to have sick leave.

This also led to more local resolutions of pay and conditions, with virtually a different scheme for every type of activity. This seemed to work fine for paying craftsmen and operatives in the outdoor world where there was strong competition, but in other areas there wasn't much competition, and so these bonuses weren't needed.

What hadn't been seen coming was that all the areas where bonuses were being paid were male dominated. The equal opportunities legislations then gave rise to the questions around, *If all those men get paid bonuses, why can't we women get paid them as well?*

When school cooks and cleaners' claims amounted to £2million in one authority, equality suddenly became a huge issue.

So with a change of government, the lot of local government could only get better. The Labour Party wouldn't want to be associated with those nasty Conservative policies would they? There must be a well thought out strategy to get rid of it all. Why yes? In a presentation to bring in the manifesto, an MP was asked what will they do about CCT, the answer was, "We will replace it with Best Value". According to legend, that was the entirety of thinking about the subject until the question had been asked.

The framework for best value has grown, got tougher, constantly changed, grown again, and then reduced a little to save money. It can be the best thing since sliced bread, or death by a thousand cuts, depending on how good you are at a sport that starts the first half as soccer, and finishes the second half as rugby, with no apparent transition, but always a 'level playing field'.

The merits of regional government still will not go away, and of course we consider getting closer to the people via neighbourhood management and parishes, with another round of local government reorganisation not far away.

There is the need to improve efficiency by 2.5% per annum under the Gershon review, and deal with an ever expanding array of legislation and guidance.

Lots of those nasty people who ran the DSOs were washed away, as all they thought about was running a business and making money. And those nice people who put the tenders out now have a business enterprise to either pass to the best bidder, or manage, but doing it our way! Now, just as we are getting used to CPA, that too will be replaced.

To be fair, a number of DSO Mangers made the cut, and the former client officers lost their jobs. One way or another there was some pain, and far too often there was the loss of crucial talent and experience from the authority.

This book looks at good practice, plus lessons to be learned, and it draws on some sporting and other analogies. Now for the strange part: This book is in fact, two books, starting at this end it is Politics or Quality? Starting at the other end it is Quality or Politics?

PoQ is focussed on legislation, Compulsory Competitive Tendering and Best Value. QoP is focussed on the mechanism of Continuous Improvement, best practice, and how to possibly re-invent an organisation.

I hope that you find that either, or dare I hope both, books are useful both now and in the future.

Dave Gaster
Director, Support Services Direct
www.supportservicesdirect.co.uk

CHAPTER ONE:

Why 'Politics or Quality'?

There is still hope that Politics and Quality can co-exist, but for that to happen, the central government politicians at all levels need to try something new. That is to start doing what they say are the right things to do in running a business correctly, their business being local.gov.uk

Let's focus on how best to do things for the customers; they are the key stakeholders for the business.

Let's work in partnership, hammer out what is wanted to be achieved, and work on getting that better.

Let's work towards empowerment, give responsibilities to the people who best understand what they do.

Let's have a strategy and framework for doing work that enables informed decisions to be made.

Let's truly work out the best ways that things can be done and share those ideas.

Let's have a five year plan that enables investment, planning and improvement.

Move away from the *one size fits all* mentality.

While that sounds a lot like Best Value wouldn't it be nice if that applied to the way central government work with local government, so that we have open and honest dialogue, with a reality to local freedoms to add value?

Best Value has a great many positive aspects, as can any long term way of working, and it has a lot of harmful ones. Take the preponderance of league tables, how much value do they add? Sure they show the teams that can play the best game, and at the end of season win the cup. Whoops sorry, they show the authorities which tick all the right boxes and may be best at what they do? Which is correct?

Leagues have been around since the late 1800's when professional football started to emerge. They were started up for rugby union and migrated out in the 1970's, probably helping generate the supreme professionality of today, with international teams at their best ever. But have they made rugby union a widely accessible game, played by even more thousands than then? Well no, but that can be blamed on the government, they encouraged so many schools to stop all those nasty competitive sports, where there had to be winners and losers didn't they. Is this another policy being actively reversed?

For there to be an upper quartile in any service, which you must aspire to; then there must be three quarters of authorities that are failing! Statistics are wonderful things! The government use them all the time, those that work for them they publicise, those that don't, get altered, so that the new base for a true comparison can realistically tell the truth.

Did you know that nearly half the schools in Britain are below the average level of performance? There's a surprise, with any normally distributed statistical comparison; there will be better than average, less than average and average. Thus almost half are worse than average, and almost half better than average. No surprises there then?

So what are the main differences between the top performers, and the bottom performers? That's the $64M question! Well the answer is not surprising!

Top performers will have: good leadership, good systems, training of key people, a good track record, a customer base that enables service delivery, constancy of purpose, good communications... So let's see a case study from one of the best performing councils according to CPA ratings.

Case Study – Best Value Review

A demanding and wide ranging contract was in an inner London borough with a variety of management issues and an indifferent history for delivering on Best Value Reviews. The borough was aspiring for an excellent CPA scoring, but the environment area had slipped the prior year from a 2 to a 1 which would inhibit any chance of progress.

The borough had recently restructured its Best Value Review Team, and was recruiting to a wider vision, it was several months into a review entitled "Cleaner Safer Places" (CSP), which needed a mixture of new impetus and professional awareness for the areas of refuse collection, Waste management, street cleansing, other area cleansing, Housing 'Caretaking' together with dealing with Anti Social Behaviour, Neighbourhood Regeneration and waste education. This was an extremely wide brief, with enormous potential for impact, covering a budget way in excess of £35M per annum.

The service director had left, and an assistant was acting up, while a variety of senior managers were either leaving, or being reorganised. Morale was very poor, and the waste manager had resigned.

The chief executive required a very positive review, as it was politically an imperative to build upon Beacon achieving transformations for other services. The council culture generally was focussed on achieving improving PI's, but the main affected directorate had a great many old school methods, and worked in a strong series of Silos, with little communication from room to room within the same sections.

There were several processes happening in parallel, some practicable ideas were tested in specific locations, new ways of communicating and cross functional teams were set up, several methods of customer consultation used, prior to, during, and after, changes to normal working.

During all this there were effectively four steering groups, one for practicable ideas, the next for performance management and Value for Money assessment (picking up best practice from across the Country), a senior management / stakeholder group, and finally a members / chief executive board.

The consultant was involved at all levels, chairing one team, (and on occasion a second), writing reports for the board, and acting as an external challenge partner to the council.

In a very short time, a significant momentum was generated, needing extreme energy and dedication from the consultant and the BV team, as well as the variety of staff who were involved with the review 'over and above their day jobs.

The learning and discovery processes were frankly astonishing, the chief executive and her immediate team, unflinching in dealing with complex issues, always demanding to achieve the best results possible, not content with simply 'a little better than now.'

The CSP review was concluded successfully with detailed implementation plans for the next three years, together with the core of service restructuring. This included a complete re-appraisal of how to deal with street cleansing, focussing on education and enforcement, rather than ever increasing budgets to clean up what's been dropped.

The service delivery was to become more localised, having generic powers and responsibilities on the streets, with close alignment to the Police at ward levels, and a lower tech approach from the contractor in many ways, from highly mechanised sweepers to, for instance people with barrows who take a pride in work.

Both members and the chief executive believed this to be the best BV Review ever conducted by the council, and it stood as a cornerstone for two bids for awards at a prestigious nationwide event.

So why did this authority have the ability to strive for an Excellent CPA score, while others languish further down the leagues? Well first of all they have ambition and a very committed, focussed chief executive.

Politically there is harmony between the management team and Cabinet, with the 'constancy of purpose' to achieve more each year. They are willing, and able, to invest in a highly professional team to work on improving the ability to do better, and to not only wring the best information out of their systems, but also to work on how they should best co-ordinate all that information and talent supporting the centre of the decision making processes.

Then they were willing to take tough decisions, and ensure they were capable of seeing them through. If something was less than good, they were willing to accept that as a fact, not simply as a criticism, and then say "How can we make it better, what will it take, and how soon can it be corrected". There was no focus on blame, simply how can we improve that?

The vision was sharp, the three year strategic plan integrated with service plans, which in turn integrated with partnering plans with the stakeholders, and various community groups. They were doing all the suggested best practice concepts from central government, and actually investing in them strongly to ensure that they worked.

When external auditors came to inspect documents, statistics, and working methods to do reality checks, there was an initial wow affect, as the council sought to market themselves in a positive, dynamic but realistic way. They also thought about the whole inspection process and prepared the ground well for it. They did their own mini inspection, saw what that told them and took action where a quick resolution was possible.

So how does this compare to a poor performing council at the other end of the rainbow for size and complexity of operations. The London borough was a major employer with around 10,000 employees, and a budget measured in £100millions, so comparing this against a very small district council should be enlightening.

The London borough could spend a fraction of one percent of their total budget, and have a very professional team for research, review, analysis, marketing, co-ordination, initiative and finance bidding.

For a very small district council which could have perhaps half of one person dedicated to meeting best practice concepts, writing Corporate Plans, and co-ordinating statistics. All the rest of the needed plans would come as part of the day job from operational staff.

So let's look at a case study from a post best value review to see how that compares:

Case Study – Post Best Value Review

This project was for a small district council which had just received a poor BV Review showing poor prospects for improvement. They had already entered into a partnering agreement with other DC's and two contractors. The head of service was away due to long term sickness.

They were running out of time to start a change from an 'anywhere on property sack collection service' to a planned wheeled bin collection with a box collection for recyclates.

The consultant was recruited to head up a project to enable top level performances within tight budgets. Within a month the scheme had been evaluated and was presented to full council where it gained unanimous support from the hung council. The specification was altered from one 240 litre bin plus one 60 litre open box, to a standard 180 litre bin, and two 60 litre lidded boxes. The price obtained for the 180's being far more competitive than forecast, enabling the change.

The purchase of wheeled bins, vehicles (refuse and recycling) plus recycling boxes were fast-tracked to conform with standing orders and European Procurement directives, while negotiations for round restructuring went ahead. The recycling vehicles were already on order via the partnership, but the final designs and layouts were considerably modified for operational and safety efficiency.

The rounds were re-structured using the council's GIS together with a database designed and built by the consultant in partnership with a small IT company. The whole process from commission to the first rounds being operational took under five months. During that time new pay and conditions were agreed with the workforce, allocations to rounds sorted, and a recycling ramp designed and constructed within the main depot

The closure of a local tip, and direction to a tip further away was potentially very difficult to bare, for both financial and operational reasons, but the DC was able to persuade the county to alter its plans so as not to jeopardise the achievements at that point. Severe weather and massive recycling participations both added pressure to the start up of the scheme.

The council agreed that there could be considerable operational flexibility to have a fixed overall nett budget, with variable resources, including the sales proceeds of the recyclates together with their recycling credits from the county, together with a considerable increase in trade refuse income (due to a step increase from wheeled bin customers, and the elimination of incorrect historic free trade services when charges should apply)

Overall the council moved from 4% recycling to 19% in a year, for no additional budget. The forecast is that the service can achieve 24% recycling once all operational and enforcement issues are settled.

The consultant was retained to carry out a restructuring review to create a streetscene service, and then to write the waste and recycling plan for the council.

The service was later commended both as part of the partnering initiative, and by IDeA with a page dedicated to it on their website.

The conduct of the council was quite phenomenal within the review, in as much that they made difficult decisions and stayed true to those decisions, even during an election campaign where such dramatic impacts on the community would have been an easy target to throw stones at supporting members.

The committee chairman acted as a conduit for local views, and worked extensively with the media, for-ever phoning and emailing the consultant on Sunday afternoons, (his usual dedicated council working time)

The service level didn't reduce during that time, and virtually all environment PI's improved dramatically as a direct result.

The performances in most managed areas were very good, they had a very close contact with the community, cleanliness levels in the streets were generally extremely good, with virtually no fly tipping, nor graffiti, grounds maintenance good, with very safe streets.

Simply reading the local papers showed how low the crime record was, with one hilarious front page news of 'Two pints of milk stolen off front door step' taking prevalence that day over the recycling roll out.

There is no doubt in my mind that this is a better place to live and work than inner London, its cleaner, safer with better prospects for education, if not employment. So why is this council rated as 'Poor', when the London borough fast approaches 'Excellent'?

Well the answer is quite clear, the London borough can afford the resources to tick every box in the Audit Commission requirements, and the district council could not. There is no doubt that the LB faced the harder tasks to do a good job, but the life qualities in the DC should have a bearing in the matter.

Therefore the question should be raised, should the Audit Commission continue to work on a 'One size fits all basis' when quite clearly it is the view of the government that councils should provide options for choice to their customers. Again should the government (and their agents) not also do as they say? Or, should a small scale 150 people establishment be compared on an equal basis to a large scale 10,000 person organisation?

CHAPTER TWO:

The Potentials to Achieve

Over the last twenty five years Britain has emerged to be one of the most successful nations in the world in a wide array of achievements.

Clearly we are a major economic power, being part of the G8, helping to steer some of the most demanding agendas the world has ever seen in peace-time. The London Stock Exchange out punches the scale of the UK to most of the rest of the world, with British economists being world class. The stability and strength of the British economy is quite staggering.

Britain also has sporting excellence, with a wide range of achievements in both rugby codes, football, cricket, tennis, athletics, yachting, martial arts...

We are among the world leaders in entertainment, with theatre, music, TV and films breaking new ground, and being box office hits. The arts are again well represented, with some of the best authors in the world.

For science and technology, we have some of the outstanding thinkers in the world, with inventions such as the world wide web being British, as well as many of the IT developments outside of silicon valley California. We lead the world in medicine, bio-chemistry and genetics.

Where-ever you look, we are doing very well, especially for such a relatively small nation, and yet we rarely celebrate our greatness. We are after all Great Britain.

We as a nation condemn failure too quickly. We don't win Wimbledon, so Tim Henman is a failure. Wow, how many people do you know that are in the top five in their profession, and you would call them a failure? We get a world champion team for rugby, and then hit them hard because of a temporary slide. Yes they could do better, but positive energy would be so much easier to harness than negative energy.

Positive energy is a very real phenomenon, I'm not a Manchester United fan, but I do admire them. When they were truly great a few seasons ago, they would win matches when they were playing badly. They would cope with having very little possession, have virtually no attacks, and then suddenly score two quick goals, and win apparently comfortably. This was because they believed in themselves, and knew that when the right chance came along that they could make it count.

Equally I have seen teams play really well and dominate the game for 70 minutes, and still lose. Why? Because they don't believe they have the right to win. When they have a good scoring chance, they can't be relaxed, they try too hard, they get nervous or tense, and so they mis-hit the shot. Most top sport is about controlling adrenalin, it can be a real boost to the metabolism, and it can pump you so high, that it's impossible to keep control.

So where does this leave service delivery within local government? Some of the best levels in service delivery happen every day, and yet are ignored. Look at rubbish collection, how often have you ever known your rubbish not to be collected? Compare that to how often you have forgotten to put your rubbish out on time, and then complained it hadn't been collected, which is the greater?

I have been putting rubbish out for some thirty odd years, with two collections a week for the last few years, (one for recycling), that's about 1,650 collections, without fail!

If I compare that to the postal service, billing from utilities, call handling by call centres, calculation of my tax, the reliability of electrical products.... The service I have received from my councils have been absolutely brilliant! Congratulations!

So let's see where that service delivery comes from, and perhaps reflect on is that 'World Class?'

Best Value introduced a series of BVPI's (Best Value Performance Indicators) which included 'Missed collections per 100,000 collections'. If I were to experience a missed collection next week, then I would have one miss in 1,651 collections, and thus a rate of 60.6 misses per 100,000. So that's a useful indicator. One failure every 30 years equates to about 60 misses out of every 100,000 intended collections.

This is one of the BVPI's that ceased being mandatory! Why on earth it was stopped I don't know, as it gave a solid comparator from place to place, although local circumstances change capabilities of systems.

I was working for a very dynamic but small district council in the early 1990's, it had moved to wheeled bin collections in 1988/89 and had one of the best services in terms of customer satisfaction in Britain. It was forced through the normal hoops of CCT in that time, succeeding to win its own contract. This created a powerful linkage at all levels within the DSO for planning work, and implementing change. Instead of resting on the laurels of good customer satisfaction, and a contract win, they decided to try to improve service delivery. (See chapter 4 (Q or P) for the full details of the process).

The management, supervisors and workforce got together and decided to analyse what caused customer dissatisfaction, and then do something about it. This was ground breaking work for us, and we could find nothing similar via reading, seminars or networking. A lot of ideas were coming in through our heavy involvement with the British Deming Association (Now Deming Forum), but all the examples at that time were about building cars and making things on production lines, not how to collect refuse better.

So we worked on the data we had, and started trying to collect data 'smarter'. Most of us didn't have PCs and couldn't use spreadsheets, so every day analysis possibilities of today weren't possible. In hindsight that was probably better, as data out of a spreadsheet in tables or graphs then may have not been taken up so well by the refuse collectors and drivers.

We analysed the data in a number of ways, and then tried to relate it to cause and effect systems. We started to learn a huge amount about what we did, and more to the point why we made mistakes! The single biggest cause of mistakes was the inappropriate use of temporary staff in holiday periods.

When we had agency staff we made vastly more mistakes. So we had knowledge, but could that help? YES, with shared knowledge, we sought a win-win solution with the collectors, if they make less mistakes, they don't have to go back and rectify them, so they finish earlier. We (the management) benefit, because there's less admin, and the council benefit as there's less fuel used, and you don't need a lot of client officers, nor switchboard staff to handle the masses of complainer phone calls… By the way, 'Quality' saves money! Something to build upon!

In 1991 we averaged 36 missed collections per 100,000, by 1993 that had reduced to 7 misses per 100,000. In 1991 we had 95% of customers satisfied with refuse collection as surveyed by MORI, at that time it was the best ever recorded. I still live in that district, the service is still excellent, so the systems are sustainable. Even with two collections a week, it should be 140 years before I may be missed.

The same ideas went with me to the neighbouring DC, they had major problems when I arrived, but they had previously been good at refuse collection. They went through changes of systems, rounds and technology, with pain, expansion, and a huge learning curve. By 2002 they were among the best in the Country with only 2.9 missed collections per 100,000. That's a likelihood of one miss every 517 years for each household collected from (A confusing 1.5 collections per property per week).

So are our services that poor in local government? How unusual are these performances? According to BVPI tables, they were not the Best in Britain, so those better places must have been absolutely mustard!

But does 'Quality' come at a cost? In general true quality saves costs, which is something that I've been trying to get through to my Son's broadband/ TV provider, if only they stopped compounding errors, they would save themselves a fortune!

The majority of people that I know, mix up specification with quality. It's the specification of a product or service that is the prime contributor to costs; the classic Rolls Royce versus Mini comparator. It is luxury (specification) which adds to costs, such as meticulously finished real timber, which has been crafted, sanded, and painstakingly varnished a dozen times will cost far more than an imitation plastic veneer.

But, that is different to the quality of the product. There are many ways to measure quality, staying on the vehicle theme, people select cars for a wide array of reasons, some of them are tangible, others less so. Thirty five years ago, most people wouldn't touch those cheap Japanese imports; they were tinny, unreliable, and rusted away. Now the same makes are among the most reliable in the world.

Here are a few ideas about why you may rank one car as a better 'Quality' than another. How many of these have you ever consciously considered when you were making a purchase decision?

Make; Appearance; Safety; Fuel economy; Braking capability; Acceleration; Top speed; Depreciation; Accessories; Reliability; Servicing costs ; Lumber support; All round vision; Impact testing.

The list isn't exhaustive, but there are many factors that help you decide what you buy, with so many factors being in the sub-conscious rather than be a logical thought out process. If there is so much sub-conscious work going on to make a tangible 'buy' decision, how many intangible areas are there when assessing a service? Where there are so many unknowns, is a league table basis the soundest for local government?

Returning to refuse collection, 'missed bins' is by no means the only factor, but it is an excellent indicator of service reliability. Refuse collection is almost an art form, a combination of people, machines and rubbish! The outcomes could bid for the Turner Prize. But the set up for refuse rounds is in fact one of the hardest logistics problems facing most management. You have so many variables to factor in, such as travel distances, weather, holidays, places and times to avoid, variable day light, seasonal load changes...

Organising 100,000 collections a week is quite a task, ensuring that the customers and services are in harmony is an even greater task. Once it's working in a certain way for about 6 weeks, then routine can return, until of course you come to a Bank Holiday, or worst of all (from a service delivery perspective) Christmas and New Year.

One thing you learn from change management for something as personal as refuse collection, is that it's impossible to make everyone happy at the same time. Changing how you deal with Christmas collections is near suicidal, even if you are doing it better than before. People are creatures of habit and don't tend to read papers, junk mail, adverts, leaflets or labels on the bins.. They don't listen to local radio, or watch local TV... Their total source of all knowledge is from the Guardian but not those nasty advert pages, and occasionally they listen to Radio 4. Yes, there are people out there who complain bitterly, because you changed collection by a day, and hadn't told them personally.

There are many ways to upset people when collecting their refuse including:

• Collecting before 7.00 in the morning
• Collecting late in the evening because
  of major (vehicle) breakdowns
• Using wheeled bins
• Not using wheeled bins
• Collecting recycling separately
• Not collecting recycling separately
• Having an innovative recycling collection
  service, as we must be conning people
• Collecting near schools around movement times
• Collecting on main roads during peak travel times
• Collecting up a narrow street by driving the lorry up it
• Not collecting from a steep road when it is sheet ice
• Not collecting from a long road when people
  have parked in such a way as to block it
• Dropping some litter
• Squeezing out some: oil, paint or liquid
  from the refuse down the street
• Being too noisy
• Arriving ten minutes earlier than usual

- Arriving thirty minutes later than usual
- Crashing into a car, when there was no collection within three miles of that point that day
- Taking stuff piled on top of the bin, not meant for disposal
- Not taking stuff piled on top of the bin.

In general for every complaint there is an equal and opposite complaint, something like Newtons' second law of motion.

I said earlier that there were 7 missed collections per 100,000 at the small DC, there were also 3 other complaints per 100,000 collections, which were also worked on. These were in descending order:

- Bin returned to the wrong location
- Missed collection at the rear of premise (Assisted Collection)
- Missed litter bin collection
- Missed sack collection
- Spillage
- Missed clinical collection
- Other?

The majority issue was part due to the specification – there was no right 'defined place' to return bins. There was no specific definition for each of the 29,000 locations. A rule of thumb was to put the bin back to where it came from, or sometimes a safer place.

Things change with bin locations, one partner in a household puts it in position A, and the other partner in position B. The collector then can put it back to B, only to have the A person complain. (Yes that does happen!).

Each round was furnished with a list of exceptions, in round order, where the assisted collections are, who has complained recently, frequently occurring faults, and so on. As the system got more mature, we also added in a 'return report' from each vehicle driver, updated hourly of bins not out. So we would have a definite record that say 7 Acacia Avenue had no bin out at 8.15, which would be pointed out at 9.15 when they rang in to say they have been missed. (That was regularly audited)

So we have a few more dimensions to delivering service quality: Specification, knowledge, communications, commitment, systems, analysis, training, staff awareness, corporate awareness, flexibility... We must be getting somewhere with all this, and thus this could be universally applied for all refuse collection, or all service delivery! Yes lots of right ingredients, and correctly used, able to make a positive difference. But not a universal panacea against all ailments, some further diagnosis is needed.

The above example was in the heady days of CCT (Compulsory Competitive Tendering), when (it is alleged) that all DSOs and contractors had only a single thought, making money! The next chapter examines some of the why's and issues of CCT, but for now it is important to note that some contracts under CCT genuinely added value to customers.

These ideas and ideals from Deming (see chapters 2 & 3 in Q o P) were rare in local government, and probably lost on anyone who manages by a fixed system, or simply manages by numbers. However, Deming was an astute statistician, and thus the current vogue of BVPI's has a great deal of affinity to some of his teaching.

Taking ideas that work in one place and applying them somewhere else is a risky business, and so a spirit of adventure, openness, and risk management is definitely needed.

The establishment of refuse rounds is shown above to be a very tricky exercise of logistics; the art of Housing Response Maintenance is even more of a daily logistical nightmare. A long term friend and Director of a Sub-contractor (he became a friend after the contract) had the dubious pleasure of taking up the balance of a huge influx of work, in what now would be described as a partnering deal.

He said that "The only reason he was able to go through hundreds of jobs worth £25.00 each, and invoice every one, was because it was his money". "How can you run a business that has to do this every day?"

Response Maintenance (RM) defies all logic of Building, Contracts and Running a Business. My DLOs would typically process about 100 jobs a day. These jobs were assigned levels of urgency; some places have say Emergency, Urgent, and Routine. At the DLO in 1992, we had 4 hour, 24 hour, 5 day, 3 week and 5 week jobs.

They were priced against a Schedule of Rates (an SoR is a description of an activity, such as take off a hinge and replace it with a new one), and there were no additional monies for emergency jobs. The district area was about 225 square miles (I still can't visualise hectares). The general nature of the client and customers is to keep bringing forward more and more 'urgency', while the contract document swears most work will be allocated at 5 weeks.

The variation from day to day was staggering, with say an average of 15 emergency jobs per day for weeks, and then suddenly 40 a day for a week, and never an apparent cause! What you could rely on in an RM (Repairs Maintenance) office is that whatever you think you are going to do this morning, it will be quite different by this evening. Work is allocated to a person or team, an emergency is brought ahead, materials off loaded, and then the emergency is far bigger, and other people are needed.

There are a string of BVPI's (Best Value Performance Indicators) for this area, and Continuous Improvement (chapters 4 & 5 in Q o P) is perfect for it. Gaining control of data is the first key. In the late 80's I helped develop a database to control Works Orders, which was later bought by ICL. (I never patented the designs). Knowledge, shared and used is power. The DLOs work grew and grew through 1991 to 1993 to such a point that the client budget became overstretched, which was a learning experience.

The performances became better, and better, we imported data electronically from the client computer system, and sent invoices back electronically. One of my favourite reports to committee was from our client, where he recorded 85% of all emergencies as complete prior to them actually raising a works order. Emergencies were phoned over, and then confirmed via a Works Order off the computer.

Another side to this work was the maintenance of void properties. A 'void' is a property that one tenant has left, and is unoccupied before the next tenancy starts. Our client officers had become interested in what we were doing, as it was better, faster, and had less problems. So they came on board with us on some of the Continuous

Improvement work on response, but in greater depth on voids, where our performance could help their targets even more.

We flow charted work, made up cause and effect charts, brainstormed some ideas, and generally all worked together as a wide partnership. (We even had contractors working next to our union convenor)

The learning was good from all sides, the client was astonished to see that the number of work processes on the DLO side for a typical works order, were three times greater than the client side. We also saw some of the constraints they had, stopping them from simply giving out work.

Voids are highly irritating, they can start on any day, but the letting starts on a Monday (Sacrosanct Monday). You could have an average of 20 voids a month, and then get 35 through in a week. There is no (statistical) point finishing any void without a tenancy agreed, so priorities change throughout the week. A property that didn't have a tenant suddenly has one, so you move from property A to B, to get that finished. This can happen several times in a week, and frequently does. This is really a situation where performances to achieve the impossible, goes before common sense.

So we came to a few conventions, all share the same data, have a single standard to work to as the finished product, enable a fast-track decision making process, agree that if something is wrong later due to the process, that it is extra work, not a penalty. {I'll explain one case, we agreed to paint wet plaster, so that property completions are brought forward, sometimes the plaster would sweat, and as a result a degree of mildew would form, that would then need to be treated and re-painted}

Performances as a whole went up, unit costs went down, customer Satisfaction increased year on year, and (aside from the budget overheating, through doing more than capacity knowledge said was possible), everyone was happy. In 1993 we were spending an average of £2,600 per void, and the average re-let period fell to 2.6 weeks. Despite working on similar systems elsewhere, that's a feat never again equalled.

CHAPTER THREE:

Why CCT in the early 80's?

The private sector lobbied successive governments for many years after the Second World War, to be given a slice of the restoration work. It then turned its attention to the infrastructure and new housing development that increased rapidly as prosperity returned to Britain. Much of this work was kept in-house by councils, carried out by internally employed workforces, particularly in the larger London boroughs and metropolitan authorities.

The 1970's had been a turbulent time for local government, with significant industrial action, and massive increases in wages. Thus when a new Conservative government came to power in 1979, something would be done about it.

The Planning and Land Act 1980 was the first of a range of demanding pieces of legislation for local government. Originally introduced as a Bill by the Labour government in 1979, ostensibly to prove that local government was better run than it was considered to be, the bill was implemented with some notable amendments on 1st April 1981. {That's when it had to be complied with}

So now certain proportions of council work had to be let to contractors, at first this wasn't too demanding, as many councils' did a mixture of 'in house work', and externally let work, so it had little affect on them. This was the dawn of Compulsory Competitive Tendering (CCT) and the emergence of Direct Labour Organisations (DLOs).

Soon the proportions of work that must be tendered increased, more work had to be put out to tender and there were rules for how work could be retained. As the impact grew on these authorities, they had to increasingly develop new ways of working, and new approaches to managing work.

In all reality many councils didn't work very efficiently then, and some twenty five years later a few still have a considerable way to go.

I headed a Highways, Sewers and Street Lighting DLO, with some 'Engineering Craftsmen' as well, 200 employees, who had never won a CCT contract, and were heavily Unionised within a council others labelled as the 'Loony Left'

There was a great deal to do, a huge amount to learn, and some battles to be played out. While the legislation creating CCT was seen as a way to privatise, there were many contractors that lost work as a result, and suppliers that suddenly lost huge margins on their sales.

I'll bring forward three examples of how things changed at that council in very significant ways in the mid 1980's:

1. The first was looking at our supplies. The borough had a well established methodology for buying supplies; there were select lists, formal long term contracts for major purchases, and a stores system to ensure we could achieve economy of scale for smaller purchases.

   Their DLO was very good at large scale reconstruction of highways, we had moved from winning no work via tender, to growing the business, reducing overheads, and winning 60% of all contracts bid for, all inside two very interesting years.

   During that process we took on a quantity surveyor from the private sector who realised the prices we were paying for asphalt and concrete were far too high. We had heard of a ring fencing arrangement for some materials, and thus suspected that the contractors were colluding to artificially increase unit costs. There were no networking arrangements with other councils, nor benchmarking to identify the problems, which proves some things have moved in the right direction since then.

   We contacted the head of finance, then the head of audit, and told them that we were about to break several standing orders and financial regulations, and wanted an auditor to stay with us for about three days to watch us doing this. Our approach was that this was in the economic interest for the council. Interestingly, when we advised of the potential saving to the borough, the concept wasn't too alien to them, and so they came and watched.

First of all we collected copies of all the formal tenders for asphalt and concrete supplies checking them for consistency. We checked to see if there were other contractors on the select lists that had not tendered, and then we compiled a list of potential suppliers.

We started phoning around to see what the prices could be on the spot market, initially with the contractors who had bid, and then increasingly with many others. We reduced the costs of these commodities by more than a third. There is no getting away from the fact that we worked a dutch auction chipping away at the tolerances of all involved. To achieve such savings we were admittedly now buying far greater volumes, but the price reductions achieved proved historic price fixing.

The reductions in costs for concrete proved to be far easier to achieve than for hot rolled asphalt. HRA needs to be very hot when delivered, otherwise its difficult to lay, and may not wear well. To prove our commitment to break the pricing rings, we eventually brought large quantities of HRA from Somerset, with it occasionally being 'a little cool' when it reached central London.

Without the spur of CCT, that exercise would never have occurred, and those savings never achieved. We addressed purchasing in a 'cut throat' aggressive and commercial manner. Prior to this event it appeared that purchasing was largely an administrative task to ensure propriety.

That single three day event saved the borough over £ ½ M in the first year, and transformed the competitiveness of the DLO. It was an historic event! We later chipped away at a number of established purchasing agreements, making significant savings, gradually taking away our reliance on the central stores.

2. Personnel issues were set in stone, there was a rigid hierarchy in the workforce of who got what promotion based on years served more than any other parameter. Most people were paid via a bonus scheme, and that was related to hard fought productivity deals, with formal organisation and management (O&M) reviews (Work study) at the core.

The protocols for work study were very much laid down, if O&M were to conduct a review it had to be pre-agreed with the unions with the individual operatives advised it was to take place. For the workforce the unions ensured that every task was to take an age, every kerb laid a work of art, with huge technical issues incurred. It really was like watching a slow motion movie.

We had to get past these games and quickly, the easiest solution was to have a profit share for each major contract, which distributed profits between the DLO and employees, with hours input providing the share calculator. Most got the idea, and the hard fought O&M regime went out the window.

Being London many people thought they could work the system, and several thought themselves absolutely 'Bomb-proof'. Some, it turned out, were bomb-proof, like the sewer worker who was registered as an alcoholic. He had a registered illness, and thus could not be disciplined for it. But, because he had to work down in excavations, he couldn't go down there because of H&S. Pursuing an economic solution to this taxed our Personnel advisors, as they had a paradox not in their guiding books. Strangely I got on quite well with the operative, and was truly saddened when we caught him stealing from stores, with sufficient evidence to make it stick.

Another person who thought he was bomb-proof was the son of the ex highways superintendent. His performances were always quite low as a Mason Pavior – he laid kerbs and paving stones – but not bad enough nor slow enough to take any action.

One day he was reported for stealing paving stones, and laying them for one of his own private customers. I conducted a review, had a hearing and sacked him. The ripples went round the yard in no time. Fancy sacking someone just for theft and doing a private job during work time, and the ex-governors son as well.

Within two days he was re-employed by appeal – not a formal system, more the old boys network. The next day he was using more of our materials finishing off the private job on our time, so I sacked him again, and no one complained.

3. Work planning and long term management of contracts had always occurred, but detailed financial monitoring had never been really needed much for the client-side, they had never spent

the full budget in a year, and always rushed through additional works in the last quarter of the year. The DLO were historically always a fairly steady pace, so there was no need for commitment accounting, nor fine tuning of accounts even on a quarterly basis.

As the DLO started to get really quite efficient, jobs were done quicker, for less money, so schemes got a little more ambitious. As the pace of work hotted up, a forum was established to monitor the trading account of the DLO, plus the available budgets within the client side.

While there was a mainframe computer system, much work to take the theory of costs to date etc, were extrapolated manually and forecasts made to project forward where we were, to assess what could be afforded. The monthly meetings were started with a distribution of paper 'management Accounts' based on the (Financial Information System) FIS reports.

Within the DLO we were nervous about projections, and the idea of receiving and discussing cold data, so we developed a series of graphs to trend various significant spending profiles, at the start of each meeting I would add today's data, and be able to comment on its validity, implications and as group, we were able to start to manage with a degree of surety.

We specified a database system to record information, and enable decision making via sound, up to date information. These ideas went to the IT department, never to be seen again.

In the second year the speed of work started to do something not expected, the DLO was working to such high performances, that not only were they going to spend more than their budget, but it was slicing large tracts out of what was expected to be done by others. A slow down was the first thought.

The two union convenors were, in their own way, magic. The council, in its infinite wisdom, had decided it was for the people. Thus it said the council would follow the instructions of its ward membership. The unions flooded the wards with new members, and took control (basically) of the council.

The DLO had difficult times, with a vast learning curve. The important fast-track changes were initiated and given momentum via the union convenors. The manager and convenors sorted out what needed to be done, the convenors told the councillors how the plans work, the councillors instructed the department management team on what they wanted, and the management team then told me what to do. It really was very efficient, a form of consensus management!

Sometimes things got more frantic than that. One morning, at 7.10am as usual I turned up at the depot to find a picket line composed of my operatives at the gates. I asked what it as about, and they were picketing to get more work out of the clients, (which we had being trying to get for months). I joined the picket line in full support of their ambitions. This was mainly me being politically sensitive, as simply crossing the line made me one of the managers who caused their problems.

They persuaded me to cross the line, so that I could start working on the problem. Within a couple of days a 'Star chamber' was assembled with the Leader of the council, councillors, chief executive, Directors, me, and an array of Union Officials.

The debate was going too and fro, but missing the point, and I was unsure of my status, nor how well ideas would be received from either side. I knew the immediate solution was to release some works outside of the bounds of the CCT legislation (Highways works in a Cemetery), which was based on my work areas prior to joining the DLO and to bring forward some 'shelved schemes' that were there should funding increase.

I wrote out a note, explaining how to crack the problem in a win – win style, and wrote at the bottom, "Wait till I have sat down again before raising this". I walked down to the end of the room and topped up my coffee, then slipped the note to the Union Leader.

I was about three strides away from him when he started blatantly reading from the sheet! It worked, and no one ever approached me about the incident.

The productivity of the whole DLO increased from £4.6M to £6.5M in two years, while the average recharges rates reduced by 14%.

The reduction was an actual saving prior to any consideration for inflation.

Even with this dramatic improvement, there were a host of issues not addressed. The capabilities of the DLO were being forever increased, and there were less suspicions of management, with an easing of the reluctance to change.

The growing pressure was that the DLOs fast increasing ability to carry out more work, increased their volume of spending, and was fast outgrowing the councils ability to fund work. The individual nature of profit sharing at a job by job level made it important for every scheme to be a winner. That in turn pressured the relationships with client officers. The DLO had far more knowledge of how streets were constructed under the wearing course than the client officers who were writing the contracts and Bills of Quantities. Thus we were able to price contracts in such a way as to be competitive, and then make money from the 'unexpected' variations.

The conditions of contract were all based on the Institution of Civil Engineers templates, and while an authority can not have a contract with its self, we went through all the usual motions, including using the Director of Public Works as arbiter.

To give him his due, he was always scrupulously fair and even handed. We won most of our cases, much to the annoyance of the client officers, where I had previously worked. After two weeks in a row of winning a case, but with reversed arguments, a case was proposed by the client that in future any argument must set a precedent for the future.

We had two cases queuing at that time, and we (the DLO) lost the first one which cost us about £1,500, I then pointed out that the queuing case thus had a precedent set, and that gained us more than ten times that sum.

There was no doubt in my mind that CCT had given a great many benefits to the borough as a whole, but it did not improve working relationships between the parties involved. A series of 'them and us' situations also started to gain momentum. The Highways DLO shared the same depot with the refuse collection service. Where we required people to work virtually the whole 39 hours a week, I had constant reminders that a refuse crew could do a full days work in 2½ hours.

There was also the union pressure to ensure everyone took their full 'entitlement' of 30 days sick leave a year, so a refuse crew could do their own round, and then go out and do someone else's round, and finish both off within five hours.

In the opposite direction the Head of Waste was having a stream of complaints from his hard working refuse collectors, who said that it wasn't fair that the Highways DLO could earn huge sums via profit sharing, and they were on a limited pay with a fixed bonus scheme. Issues were stirring that would feed into the equality of pay arguments in the near future.

While the pressures were mounting internally, the government were not satisfied that they had done enough to deal with their local government problems, only a small proportion of work was actually going out to the private sector, and often now with reduced margins. DLOs were either successful and grew, or occasionally feather bedded to save too many draconian actions.

The commercial acumen and thinking of the good DLOs didn't need to pervade the vast majority of the council. Thus the central core of LA's went on working as usual. Some of the very forward thinking DLOs actually started bidding, and working for other councils in what became known as cross boundary tendering (CBT). A ruling was later made on behalf of the Audit Commission strongly implying that CBT was in fact illegal, as it infringed the 1970 Goods and Services Act. While that view was heavily espoused by government and the Audit Commission on their behalf, they studiously refused to take legal action against those Authorities who ignored them.

Considering all the above the wider intentions of the P&LA 1980 had not made enough of an impact on local government, nor for the private sector to gain 'government' work, so the Local government Act 1988 started to take shape.

CHAPTER FOUR:

Were DSOs right for the Nineties ?

In hindsight I would agree that both the 1980 and 1988 Acts were, overall, good things for the British economy helping to start the much needed transformation of local government. Both these Acts could have been designed to have more benefit to customers, and be less of a burden on previously well performing services, which is why, to some extent 'Best Value' is now in place.

Hindsight is a wonderful thing, but the lack of information, quality control, and abysmal levels of productivity per person 25 years ago were totally indefensible.

I was recently talking with three senior Accountants about the affects of a new Pay and Conditions scheme for their workforce. They were 'traditional' accountants and could see the increase in the cost of pay, and thus believed it to be a failure. I was trying to argue that the increased costs had been planned, and they could only occur where there was an even greater increase in productivity, and thus there was a reduction in unit costs of work done, as the fixed costs were dissipated over a larger base.

Well I'm not an accountant, but to me the position was crystal clear, you had the same number of people doing more work, with the same vehicles and management structure, so as pay increased, real unit costs decreased. To convince them I had to build quite a sophisticated spreadsheet, initially with an indicative budget, and then a real one.

When I reflected on this, the reason this was crystal clear to me, was that I had been doing this for over 20 years, and they were straight forward 'bread and butter' concepts. To them it was a totally unrehearsed paradigm that must include some sort of trickery.

Anyway, the initial influences of the 1980 Planning and Land Act had some impact on larger councils, but even there it was no certainty that there was not any real gain in Value for Money terms, nor was there an overall decrease in work done in house. Some DLOs did get smaller or were shut down, but many others got bigger, and gained a market share from the private sector. As discussed there was also a probable decrease in margins for major building and civil engineering contractors due to the increased vigour and competitiveness of the emerging DLOs. The margins for suppliers also would have reduced as a result of more effective procurement, rather than the previous administration style of buying.

The whole construction industry went into a recession for a long while, which admittedly started in the mid-70's. The increased opportunity to compete for local government work did not seem to help the contractors out of that recession. The construction industry pulled back significantly from any longer term internal development actions, higher education places for construction related professions reduced, with it being almost impossible to get placements for students and newly qualified graduates.

Since that time there has also been far less investment in skills training for the future, the private sector had plummeted into a deep recession where survival was paramount, and the fledgling DLOs became very cost conscious with profits needing to be achieved for the first time. Historically local government had been a major source for the long term training needs of the Construction industry, once financial pressures started to really bite, that area quickly dwindled.

As a direct result, there has been a twenty five year slow down in training for a whole host of trades, such as Roadworkers, Paviors, Electricians, Plumbers, Carpenters and Bricklayers. Apprenticeships virtually disappeared, and a whole generation of skills was lost. Many companies and organisations have started to address this, but it's not unusual to find the average age of a skilled workforce to be approaching 50 years old. New issues always arise out of change, this one has been a long time coming, and will take even longer to go away.

Is the capability for a plumber to do his sharp intake of breath, and say "That will be £75.00 plus £35.00 an hour" due to these Acts? If not entirely, it must have something to do with them! Electricians in London earn anywhere up to £100,000 a year. If there wasn't the scarcity of skills, the costs would be far less. So has CCT actually directly contributed to recession and inflation? Is that why Wembley Stadium is three times dearer than its counterparts across Europe and Japan?

The 1988 Local Government Act was better drafted for bringing in changes, and had learned from some of the disruptive capabilities from the 1980 Act. This again was to be phased in, with all Authorities having to address CCT, with a proscribed roll out plan, such that competition could be gradually taken up by the private sector, with quite strict guidance on how big, or small tranches of work could be, plus what could be done at what time, with a view to stopping an overload in any one area for any one type of work.

For instance street cleansing contracts would be introduced in 1990 for one council, 1991 for the next and so on. In general there was a five year gap from first to last. If 1994 was the street cleansing year for a council, refuse collection could be in 1991, grounds maintenance in 1992 etc.

The target dates for each council were mandated, and it had no bearing at all on needs, urgency, capability or value for money. Local authorities had to do this or face retribution.

The 1988 LG Act affected district councils in a big way introducing CCT, often for the first time, where for most DC's, the 1980 Act was no more than inconvenient mainly; the impact on larger authorities became very significant. Services included: refuse collection, street cleansing, grounds maintenance, building cleansing, catering, vehicle maintenance and Leisure Services.

Now the new age of contracting took to life. The construction industries had more than a century of experience in writing and tendering for contracts. Those conditions of contracts were well developed, and specifications honed to perfection...

There was no expertise to write a good refuse collection contract, but a new industry was blossoming. Many Authorities worked together to build a useful contract. The pioneers in the first phases went out with best endeavours, and the latter phases borrowed, learned from and improved upon these works of art.

Where all this work had previously been done 'twin hatted', within amorphous departments such as environmental health or parks, they now had to be split up. There were the legal teams, the accountants, administrators, and then the client (who says what is to be done, and monitors it) and the contractor, either in house or external.

In most cases the contractor elements were joined together to give a centre of expertise, these became the councils DSO. (The 1988 act had direct service organisations, as opposed to the direct labour organisations of the 1980 Act) There tended to be areas in the country where competition was fierce, for instance in the south east and coastal towns for refuse collection, while in other areas where there was little or no competition at all.

The setting up of DSOs also affected councillors, they could not be involved in the whole cycle of letting, bidding for, and award of contract, so a new form of declaration of interest and division of responsibilities emerged.

This was a long term thorn in running committees and boards. The *client side* councillors would forever ask contractor related questions, and the *contractor side* would forever challenge the specification of works.

A whole chapter could be written on the corporate running of a business inside a council. Far too often it just couldn't be right. Then there are the Politics, (this time with a capital P). I had one board chairman who would regularly reflect out loud, "I wonder what Maggie would do about this?"

The Conservatives were split, should they applaud the fact that their own DSO can be extremely competitive, be good risk takers, and take extra work via competition, or should they resist any option other than private sector doing everything. Having both factions on the same board was interesting, and dependant on who attended, it could be very like Animal Farm, were four legs better than two?

To keep the balance, labour councillors liked having a DSO in general, but didn't like them being too commercial, particularly where operatives had to work far harder to stay in business. In each DSO I built an escape plan early on. This would be a workers co-operative option for Labour and a management buyout for Conservative. In the end they were remarkably similar! I also worked for a Liberal Democrat council, which was, on balance, more at ease with the DSO, and that enabled it to be virtually like running a business.

There was also a great deal of rumour around large multi-national companies taking up these contracts as 'loss leaders' in a longer term desire to have more profitable contracts in the second round of competition. These contracts were not, generally, highly lucrative, and thus the industry sought ways to make relatively expensive, loss making or low profit, contracts more worthwhile.

Some achieved a greater return by substantially altering the pay and conditions of staff, such that the total weekly pay was perhaps retained, but far more work had to be carried out to earn that sum. Holiday entitlements would be reduced, and sick pay greatly altered.

Increasingly a little known piece of European law emerged to cover transfers of staff from one organisation to another, as a transfer of business. This is TUPE, the transfer of undertaking and protection of employment regulations. This was to some extent an unknown, with the holders of work and employees able to decide whether it applied or not. Various precedents were achieved altering views as they came and went. A degree of latitude is still left with the new employer, such that they could change the terms of employees due to 'Economic, Technical or Operational' reasons after transfer. Yet another change of interpretation is expected early in 2006.

Some major players with a host of transferred employees would collect dozens of differing schemes, making the payroll and personnel systems cumbersome. They also faced another law giving everyone the right to challenge their payment schemes under equal opportunities. Clarity and a pecking order of which was most important were needed. Eventually law was made to further clarify these issues.

In time there were many contractual gains for the private sector, plus an amazingly strong collection of surviving DSOs. In many places these DSOs sought to work for other authorities, or even the private sector. Many were stopped either by their own authority, or after grim warnings from external auditors.

The reality of Cross Boundary Tendering (CBT) was never really tested. According to a relatively junior barrister CBT infringed the

1970 Goods and Services Act, in that no council should do work for an other to gain profit. It seemed strange that the 1888 Local Government Act foresaw the need for one council to do work for another, as centres of expertise would grow, and that charges should apply between them.

Most of those who did do work for others did it in a very commercial way, creating local employment, and either bringing in profits to the council as an additional funding source, or enabling current budgets to be spread a little wider. Many of these were based in the North of England, with a few elsewhere. One of the most dynamic and successful is a home counties borough council, with its apparently 'free market' DSO bringing in over £4M worth of work a year, significantly subsidising its authority's prime activities.

This borough was 'leaned on' several times to stop this work due to transgressing the CBT instructions of the Audit Commission, but neither the government nor the Audit Commission ever took this to a judicial review. Two successive directors of this service went on to become chief executive, which underlines the commercial value of a well run DSO.

A south west council approached me in the late nineties regarding several performance and operational issues. They realised that we were carrying out work that their auditors wouldn't let them do under the Goods and Services Act interpretation. They were surprised that my head of legal had determined it as totally OK, and even more surprised I could give them a copy of another QC opinion that it was in deed legal.

They explained that they had set up and successfully operated a uPVC double glazing factory, and had capacity to make more windows and doors than needed for their council. The external auditors and then internal audit forbid them making these products for any other authorities. Thus their unit costs bore very high overheads, and were not as good as they could be. The political influence here, as in many parts of the country drove up prices, not only for that council, but most likely for their neighbours as well.

With the maturing systems there became increasing opportunities to work with others and learn from each other. Two major organisation

4: Were DSOs right for the nineties ?

emerged representing DSOs, there was ADLO (The Association of Direct Labour Organisations) which was largely Scottish in origin, and initially very heavily politically orientated, hell bent on fighting legislation at first. This now has transformed into APSE, (The Association for Public Sector Excellence). As 'APSE', it has broadened its range, influence and public acceptability.

The other was started in the South East and was called ACSCO, (The Association of Contract Services Chief Officers), which also has grown in influence and changed name to PSnet, (The Public Services Network).

Both of these run regular seminars, networks and benchmarking services. Being both a southerner and not very political, {I attack any party that brings in half thought through ideas with equal vigour}, I have been a member of PSnet for quite a few years, regularly sitting in the front row to deeply question the latest government speaker.

The value of net-working has grown, so that you don't have to re-invent the wheel, there is virtually always someone out there who has tried an idea out and learned from it. Additionally the benchmarking data can be invaluable to influence your service plan, or Best Value action plan.

We should return to the affects of all this tendering for work in the early 1990's, and how that affected the people and organisations which had for years been doing this work. In general the status quo of doing municipal work had not changed much in 90 years. There had been major changes to local government in the early 1970's with larger district councils replacing almost three times the number of Town and Rural DC's. But the workers went on, with bosses vying to get a job, or even promotion.

The good old GLC was also ousted as an embarrassment to the then government, especially as County Hall was straight across the river from the Westminster Gas Works (Houses of Parliament).

So this division of power and re-organisation was the biggest change ever to affect those people who come into contact with the public on a daily basis. (Dare I say it, the Blue Collar Services), its strange how personnel terms change, although are they all staff, members, employees, cast members or what?

45

CCT often shuffled the financial pack, but rarely made the budget cheaper. In the olden days the works unit would have had a set budget and everything came out of that. Most accounts were fairly linear, so next year's budget was the same as last, with inflation added on. There was harmony, control, and the gradual trickle affect from new technology, such as faster, bigger, heavier Lorries.

If you needed fifteen rounds to collect refuse, you may have 18 vehicles, 67 operatives, a manager, supervisor, and an admin officer. There would be a garage, and all repairs would be done there, with a manager and three fitters. Job done!

Under CCT this all changed. You could do the work with less rounds, with less people on each vehicle, but even more high tech vehicles, that needed expert maintenance. The DSO would need an overall manager, an accountant, and admin support. The refuse manager would need an assistant, and two admin staff to deal with the instructions and requests from the client. All these processes would have to be recorded in the new IT system. In addition you needed a new post to achieve ISO 9002, 14001 and IiP demanded in the contract documents.

The client would have a contracts manager, and two customer services officers, to take calls from the public, and relay them to the contractor, raising default notices, and instructions as need be. They also needed their own computer systems to monitor and control work. Everything became more formal, complex with a string of duplications. Officer numbers increased and operative numbers decreased. Both the client officers and the DSO would be part of separate reporting lines to committee / board members, both reporting on performances and finance, while the former should concentrate on specification, customer care and strategy, and the latter on operational achievement and implications.

Then you had several layers of auditors, those checking accounts, then systems, and later BVPI's. I had three audits affecting my Building Maintenance DLO in three consecutive years. The first started from stores and supplies, the second from payroll, and the third as an audit of works order validity and variation. Each report stated that the filing system for the Works Orders should be kept to match the theme of the audit. We retained the only logical idea, which was different from all three audits, keep them in numerical order!

Overall there became less people actually collecting refuse, and therefore working harder, and a new battalion of office staff lobbing invoices, instructions, and counter instructions at one another. Where-ever this was an in house contract, the whole paper-chase was based on a theoretical contractual situation that has no legal bearing (A council can not have a contract with its self!)

Forgive the cynicism, where there was a good operation in place, prior to competition, there was a good chance that the overall costs would increase, but where there was a borough with an average of 30 days sick leave a year for all staff, and a 2½ hour working day, there were millions of pounds to be saved every year.

I worked at a borough recently where a third generation refuse collection contractor was just being appointed. The outgoing contractor had only just got to terms with trying to eradicate those old problems. The first refuse contractor had started the process, and lost monies in the battle, as had the second. Is this a case of third time lucky?

There are so many viewpoints within all these matters that it can make your head swim. I was discussing the merits of DLO to Private Sector employment within the refuse industry with the General Secretary of a major union, he said that one of the best factors within the private sector, which his membership really thought was much better than for Public Sector was that they dismissed people who just couldn't or wouldn't work properly. "You know where you are with these people, they are there to do a job and make money. These councils that are afraid to sack someone cause major problems for the workers alongside the lazy ones"

DLOs often seemed to be working to a different agenda to the Corporate Core. Personnel is one of those variable feasts, some councils recognise that being 'tough' is beneficial to the majority of employees, others go ultra soft (Cautious) making it nearly impossible to take positive action where it is needed.

One personnel officer was defending the sub-division of procedures from one line of disciplinary into three discreet areas, with an

A4 folder about 10 cm thick to run them, and concluded that the Refuse management structure was too lean to manage the workforce correctly. That particular team had won awards, and was producing world class operational results, with low costs and absenteeism, but an increasing issue with discipline. She could not see that their policies were damaging service delivery.

The worst aspects of CCT and BV is that they are both broadly a "One size fits all system", everyone has to tender their service sometime. If the service quality is excellent, and the costs per operation are low, competition is still needed by law but not by common sense.

With tools like best value and benchmarking, would it be best to say: With this specification, and these parameters, you need to tender work only if your contract exceeds £x per property? Then the randomness is taken out of the equation, only those that are benchmarked as expensive need to tender, those that give value for money are exempt.

Other background issues abound behind the simple aspects of CCT; in 1990 the Environmental Protection Act came into force, helping transform the majority of British streets into a far cleaner existence than before. Housing law has changed repeatedly making it for ever harder to keep social housing in local government.

But the waste industry is probably the recipient of the greatest increase in legislation than anything else in Britain. European legislation has forced an ever increasing pace to divert waste from landfill, massively increase recycling, deal with clean air, abandoned cars, end of life vehicles (recycling), WEEE regulations (electrical equipment recycling), fly-tipping, littering, graffiti, etc.

Every time legislation changes, several thousand contracts for waste, recycling, street cleansing, housing maintenance etc need to be reviewed and often renegotiated. Add to this employment law and Health and Safety law, and you have an ever increasing expertise needed in law, and contract law for each and every council. If the law changes and you have an in house team carrying out a 'Contract', you can often change the contracts with no or little expense.

If it's a contractor doing the work, and that contractor under-bid the contract in the first place, then contract renegotiations become a life blood towards profitability.

I've addressed two contracts where the client had to do something different as a result of a change in strategic or legal requirements; in the first one the contractor had a long term contract (15 years) and then the council needed to radically increase recycling diversion to meet mandatory government targets. After a great deal of discussion, with insufficient paper-work, a financial agreement was hammered out, such that over the 15 year period the contractor would pro-actively work on recycling, achieving a considerable diversion of waste by the end of the period.

The deal was done, and the alteration to contract agreed, and the client started to make additional payments as scheduled. After a short while the client was concerned that there were more costs, but no changes in recycling. Despite the agreement being quite clear on when payments were to be increased, it was only the year 15 position that needed to be achieved for recycling and up to year 15 the contractor could be paid more, for the same! This was later resolved after considerable legal work, negotiation and more than a little adverse publicity.

In another case the borough had tendered a refuse contract and offered the use of depot free of charge with an ability to terminate that use at any time. The contract started quite well, and a redundant building at the depot was added, enabling a proactive increase in recycling at an agreed fee.

The borough was cash starved, and so needed to sell its Depot, which was far too big for its remaining workforce, and had planning permission for a rather nice housing development. The refuse contractor was given notice to quit, and they immediately submitted claims for the prime contract, and the recycling subsidiary.

This was unresolved for four years, the contractor had found a potential depot, and achieved planning permission with some works, and moved to it quite quickly. Understandably there was an increasing tension between the two parties, and hence a move to litigation for over £¾ M with one or two other issues.

Interestingly the claim for the loss of a recycling facility held more substance, as the agreement had been written by the contractor. After a form of mediation, the contractor grudgingly agreed to settle for a sum £600K less than the starting position. The contract had otherwise been running in a quite amenable fashion, to a good standard, but the higher level dispute had strangled innovation and trust out of the relationship. Hence the potential for being better had been lost.

These two examples show how important the contractual relationships must be. If either party is too strong, then there will be no give and take, nor working to a mutual benefit.

Another theory, which in places is proven by outcomes, is that CCT destroys the quality of work. Many Clients got what they specified, and that cut both ways. Consider the implications of a street sweeping contract for rural areas. There are mile after mile of channels (the strip between the kerb and road, often called the gutter) that needs sweeping. One client said these would be 'totally clean' after sweeping. There was no definition, nor measurement technique to determine what was 'totally clean', it was intended it meant the same standard for channels swept daily as for those swept quarterly. Clearly a client who had never used a vacuum cleaner at home!

Some of these channels hadn't seen a sweeper ever, and were 5 cms deep in detritus, (that's contract speak for dirt), there were weeds that had rooted in a previous generation with a tenacity that a wire brush had little impact on. These channels were to be totally clean after the first sweep, and after every 3 monthly sweep there-after. You can imagine the RSM going out with his white gloves to check for discolouration.

So as the contractor you had two approaches, bid £4.5M and lose the contract, or 'qualify' the contract, and bid £500K. You could lose a contract for pointing out your interpretation of clean, or how soon it could be achieved. To say the least a good number of contracts were awarded to firms who couldn't do them as specified. And there were a good number of specifications that couldn't be afforded.

Making a workforce do more work for the same money isn't always an easy area to address! When you add that to substantial working practice changes you have an interesting recipe for problems.

I headed the only Refuse DSO in the County; all the other contracts had been awarded to the Private sector. After a while I was invited to an informal forum of private sector contract managers, where they usually compared notes about the aspirations of Clients, and often had a laugh about the money made on these little extras.

Within a year of one another, two neighbouring refuse collection contracts were tendered and awarded to new contractors. The first one was worth several million pounds over the seven year contract term, and the existing contractor had been performing quite well. The new contract would save the council a few thousands pounds over seven years.

It started horrendously, out of 60,000 collections a week, they were failing to collect from 10,000 homes, the debacle went on for weeks; the situation wasn't getting better. The press were having a field day, criticising the council for every aspect of the deal. The council went to their previous contractor to see if they apologised they would take the contract back, with no success. Then that council approached my DSO, as we had the best performances in the area. We recognised a poisoned chalice and thanked them for the offer, but respectfully declined it.

That took literally months to resolve, cost councillors and officers their jobs, and did no favours to anyone. So then the next authority proceeded to tender their work.

We already had been experiencing difficulties in retaining operatives, as it was an area of full employment, with a great deal of well paid labourers on building sites. Most council's and private sector contractors in the area were having severe difficulties in recruiting and retaining anyone for refuse, recycling or street cleansing. So any act of taking over a successful contract, and changing at all, would need careful forethought, local knowledge, and a great deal of tact.

We had moved the contracts for employment of our workforce to a 37 hour, 4 day week, with an option to work the fifth day at flat rate, from the more conventional 39 hour, 5 day week. In reality it gave a potential 25% pay rise for longer hours, or an extra day leave every week. We had no problems retaining staff as a result. This made the individual refuse rounds an average of 18% more effective, (it's a long story!)

At the second authority the performance of the previous contractor had been excellent, being a pathfinder locally for recycling, with a good level of local public support. The new contractor knew how to do this all better, for far less money, and convinced a knowledgeable council that it was fully capable to deliver new ways of working, and that it would improve services and reduce costs.

The new ideas were to have single vehicles with a longitudinal split (a division the whole length of the body), so that waste goes to the left and recycling goes to the right. This meant that all rounds had to change on the same day. That all of the customers had to change how, and often when, they put both materials out, and then instead of having two lots of crews covering the district, there would be only one.

There were a few teething problems! Not all the vehicles were available on day one, many of the vehicles had annoying bedding in problems. Recycling rates varied considerably from place to place. In some areas the recycling volume of the vehicles would fill first, in other areas the refuse would fill first, either way leaving much of the vehicle empty, and thus causing more trips to tip, and then causing the workers to finish later and later.

The workers, always wishing to help in these situations, found a solution to their problems; they would mix some of the recyclates in with the refuse, so they could get round their area with as few trips for tipping as possible. This of course was seen by the public, press and councillors... and the air turned blue! There were thousands of complaints, articles in the press, refuse piling up all over the place, and devastation to their PI's.

Much the same as a few months before them, this council hadn't evaluated the risks of change properly, and as they hadn't got an in house service, they hadn't the expertise to evaluate the risk of such changes.

By 1997 there was a degree of stability in the workings around and within CCT, with a fairly well established set of contracts, DSOs and contractors living in some degree of harmony, client Divisions who worked well with their contracting counterparts, and a move towards improving standards with Value for Money as a result.

Customer panels would give feedback on the performances of contractors, councillors had a fair idea who to approach about what. So it must be time to replace all this with something far more intrusive into the whole council, Best Value was given life!

4: Were DSOs right for the nineties ?

CHAPTER FIVE:

Was it right to move to Best Value in the Noughties?

OK you're right, Best Value started late in the 90's, but I still like the sound of the 'noughties' and I decided to go for a little poetic licence. Its strange in a way that we are now deep into the 'Naughty noughties' and yet this is one of the most Politically Correct Eras in history, if not prim and proper, certainly a period that may be remembered for protecting the perpetrators of crime, rather than the victims of crime. Still what comes around, goes around!

Best Value has a great many positives about it. It forces all aspects of council work to come under the microscope, it brings in Performance management, the four C's of Compare, Compete, Challenge, Consult; and it brings in Continuous Improvement. Where the previous two Acts had affected only small parts of the whole, this goes the whole way, well hopefully it will.

Starting with the CPA process, (Comprehensive Performance Assessment) in chapter one I introduced two Case Studies, the first from a massive, aspiring inner London borough, the second from a minute district council. There is no doubt that the latter area has by far the better quality of life, and that the former is better managed, and improving quicker.

I worked in each of them for several months, nearer to the chief executive in the borough, but having more direct influence on the district. Yes the borough is better managed, but for one to verge on Excellent, and the other be Poor is a travesty. It would appear that much of the CPA process measures the ability 'To do Best Value', rather than to provide appropriate value for money services.

The two really are chalk and cheese, 25,000 people living in 350 square miles served by about 150 staff, against 210,000 people living in about 6 square miles served by several thousand staff. The borough has a wealth of very educated staff, run professionally generating reams of reports, plans, partnerships, projections and so forth. It is a highly complex piece of big business, and is run as such.

To prepare for an inspection the borough has a team of people to bring together all the required documents, to vet them, to improve them, and then present them in a professional and polished format. There is time and resource to ensure that any foreseeable document or supporting evidence is available, and all of these compare and cross-relate to every other document.

The district needs to produce almost an identical array of documents, accepting that the range of services they deliver are less. These documents need to also be able to provide a foundation to ensure all services are legal, with good plans for the future and delivered well. There is probably half a post for co-ordinating these, and otherwise, they are drafted by operational managers and Directors.

When an inspector calls to that borough, there will be every courtesy, resource and facility available. The inspector is important to them, and will be treated as such. This is not a criticism, purely a matter of fact. There is no attempt to pervert the course of justice, favours neither asked for nor offered.

Prior to the inspector calling there is an intense period of preparation, rehearsal, possibly a mock inspection, a Challenge Partner from outside will look with fresh eyes to see what is wrong, and see whether that can be rectified realistically.

At the DC, there may be a room, and call upon someone when needed. The operational Head of Service would have prepared all the documents needed, spoken with staff in preparation, and effectively allowed the inspector to review the day to day reality of their systems.

There is no point in comparing a village shop with the whole of Tescos, nor a lock-up garage with Toyota, but that is what the CPA system is attempting, and failing to learn from its own lessons.

Deming developed a 'profound Knowledge', which few people will ever be aware of, however, his thoughts and teachings are supported by the Department of Trade and Industry (go to their website, and type Deming into their search facility). One of his profound statements is "That the most important things to know about a business are unknown and immeasurable."

Comparisons are fine, but shouldn't a degree of proportionality or 'Fit for purpose' come into the Audit Commissions thinking? As I said, it would appear that much of the 'what' CPA measures, is the ability to do Best Value, and not to deliver VfM services. As repeatedly raised they have a system based on 'One size fits all', but it clearly does not.

Let me explain. By 'Do Best Value' I am referring to reading through all the documented needs, seeking all the terms, KPI's, BVPI's, 4C's... and to pull them into an integrated well presented portfolio. Whereas achieving excellent public services is giving the public what they need, when they need it, in a reliable, no failures way.

Does the public want its bins emptied quietly, cleanly and regularly, or do they want to see a tome that details how it is done, and what measures kick in when various events occur. It's the practice that the Public are interested in, not the theory!

I'll leave the CPA there for now, as I've already touched on league tables, which I thought were a bad thing for Rugby Union in the 70's.

Now let's look at the affects of Best Value operationally, mainly within the area where CCT had come to some degree of maturity prior to BV.

The prime affect in many councils has been to sweep away the client/ contractor splits and re-integrate roles, this time making some of the senior officers, and administration redundant, as you clearly don't need to separately handle these calls with an intricate game of cat and mouse in the middle.

It is fairly random who survived, and who was lost. Some of the decisions were Political in nature, others focussed on retirement ages, and some, unsurprisingly were dealt with methodically on merit.

Inheritance can be a difficult area to deal with. client officers inheriting a DLO suddenly have a very large number of people to 'Manage' on their JD, and those staff tend to think in a different way to the client. They tend to work longer hours, be more flexible, and a little less predictable than 'your usual office dweller'. They also have a stronger sense of opportunism, and if the new manager hasn't the old restraints that 'we must make a profit on this contract, or we will go under' gives, then maybe, just maybe, there could be more money for doing less.

On the other side, the ex DLO manager, can not only inherit 'those lazy staff that only ever did armchair surveys', but suddenly also gets 30 year plans, capitalisation of works, tenant forums...

These respective roles have been developing separately for up to twenty years or so, so the sudden loss of either party can come as more of a blow than an organisation may have suspected. In the refuse industry as a whole there is an ever increasing legislation burden, more officers going into the private sector than ever, and many people retired early on a good package.

In short, there is a tremendous gap between supply and demand. Councils need environmentally & economically aware waste officers, but there simply are not enough to go round. Some of these are now earning as much as an Electrician in London. Only they don't need to be in London, the shortage is national. Is this another of those foreseeable events arising out of national change?

Under the new BV system many Authorities reviewed their direct services prior to internal services, as they, (the DSOs) were used to that sort of process and could cope better, or simply because the political pressure to move back to twin hatted was far too great.

Very few of the 're-integrated services' that I have been involved with, or have discussed with their management have done much, or anything about the 'C' with the most coverage when the four 'C's' were first floated: Compete!

Compete?

There is a hope that good BVPI's and a little benchmarking may suffice to keep the auditor happy. Some councils can show how much cheaper they were than the other contractors, 8 years ago, and then perhaps can project onto that the economy savings of merging the client contractor elements together. In general one of the biggest fears since CCT finished is that too many people have lost the art of competition.

One housing association I spent some time with was very clever, and had received the tick in the box from external auditors. They were a medium sized HA, with a very large geographic area, a good steady and astute chief executive, with a commendable approach to Personnel, H&S, and customer care.

They had their own DSO, with a very good supplies partnership, and evolving IT solutions. They mainly worked on their own properties, but had four contracts for other HA's with properties in their area. They had proven "Competitiveness" to the auditor by demonstrating they had been awarded these four contracts after competition, and that their own in house recharges were no dearer.

I pointed out to the DSO manager that he had several thousand homes within a reasonably close proximity to each other, and that each of these external contracts was based on a few dozen properties over the same area. I told him I would add at least 15% to standard rates for that situation. He looked at me and said, "So would I, but we've been doing this for years, and no one else saw what you realised!" *Does this prove what I have always suspected, that most BV auditors only seek ticks in boxes, and don't even try to understand most of the business?*

Another HA had asked me to carry out a Best Value Review to sort out some of their operational issues, and prepare them for expansion via winning work for others. They were an extremely well performing HA, with a string of good BVPI's and slightly better than average costs according to benchmark feedback.

Ostensibly they should be needing little help nor surgery, please consider the following:

Case Study ~ Housing Maintenance

A well performing medium housing association in the Midlands wished to grow the scale and scope of their DSO, but had some major problems to overcome. They recruited a consultant to deal with a number of issues, and then increased the scope of the review as an extension of contract.

The core process was driven as a 'Business Regeneration Process', introducing new practices, and improved ways of working, at the same time it was to act as a Best Value Review, including all of the fours C's. The problems to address at first included: 4 sets of pay and conditions for the workforce needed change and integration, to help specify the replacement of the Computer System which was to be no longer supported by its supplier, to move out of the Depot to a new stores site nearby, and to address competitiveness via Benchmarking and improved financial control measures.

The Pay & Conditions area was the most pressing as it was causing significant pressures for management and Administration alike, together with animosity between operatives earning dissimilar sums when working together. A number of resolutions had been tried over the previous seven years, never quite getting a full sign up, and simply creating an additional scheme.

Within two months the Board and whole Workforce had signed up to a 'Competency based scheme' broadly aligned to their officers scheme. They had tried to implement other ideas before without success, wanted a system that underpinned high performance with control, and enabled greater competitiveness.

The scheme had four components of: Skills Matrix, Quality, Training and Productivity. The scheme would improve productivity and flexibility, enabling growth while reducing the burden on management and Administration. The system went live a month later, and was de-bugged while all the historic work rounds were gradually identified and removed.

The planned move to a remote store was reviewed for costs and operational impact, and as a result was abandoned. The plans were changed to create a Sub-store alongside the HQ, and enter into a supplies partnering arrangement, with an EU compliant process for award. The supplier not only prices against pre-agreed core items, but also delivers to the sub-store by 8.00 daily, delivers to voids and major works, sets aside materials for collection within 30 minutes of order, and works to improve material supplies with a 50/50 savings plan.

The computer system turned out to be far better than described, and after some minor adjustments and improvements turned out to be very good for the job. By chance the supplier had also agreed to maintain it in the future, and thus the £270,000 replacement plan was shelved. The Response Maintenance officer had daily reports showing emergency needed by today, urgents by tomorrow, and routine by next week. The already high performances moved to 100% on time for the first time ever within three months.

The system also had extremely good capabilities for interconnectivity, thus hand-helds for supervisors and surveyors were approved and started to implement, with a latter plan for full E enabled Works Order raising and completion by operatives. The partnering arrangements for the supplies also was specified to electronically send orders, receive goods and handle the invoice for goods.

A Stakeholder meeting identified major growth potentials with a partnering possibility for an extra £2M turnover per annum. A tenants meeting identified a very content position other than dealing with communications. Partly as a consequence the Call Centre operation was added to the brief and a simple solution to achieve 90% of single call handling to achieve an appointment, or notice of emergency works was achieved.

- *A proposal for a new structure was agreed which with new technologies would enable 35% growth of business, at no cost.*
- *A vehicle replacement policy was introduced saving some £13,000 a year alone.*
- *The business planning process identified £700K of internal growth, and £2M of external growth.*
- *Performance management was addressed showing significant gains by re-addressing the use of data.*

Within all of this, one of the biggest surprises was their lack of awareness of their cost of service. They used the National Housing Maintenance Forum SoR's to pay some of the workforce, and for their 'notional' trading account. Historic records showed that when they entered prices into benchmarking comparators, that they simply used the above prices with an overall percentage adjustment, to reflect the notional accounts.

With some work the team would be ready to compete, for the small fry at first, and then move on to some very interesting options. The two lead officers in the team were trained QS's (Quantity Surveyors), their lack of inquisitiveness frankly astonished me. With all that professional training, they never had taken a real interest in costs?

Compare

The same HA had never tried to work out their own costs for any one of the SoR's and thus had no idea of the competitiveness in any one trade, and due to the array of pay schemes, could not hand on heart say how much any one job cost them.

When the two sets of benchmarking surveys, which had been 'used' for several years, were checked, neither added value, one was so 'light' operationally as to be useless, the other had a whole series of transposed data in it, such that differing entries for the same SoR could have £2.37 and £123,943.76 for the same line. It was shambolic, and had never been noticed by the operational management, nor the performance manager. In short the exercise was a tick in the box for the auditor, with no attempt to add knowledge through the intelligent use of sound information.

The value that good benchmarking can add to an organisation is considerable. How can you act on your weaknesses, if you don't know what they are, and how can you build on your strengths?

This isn't the case in all places, at the inner London borough, where most services were out-sourced via several rounds of competition, it was very difficult to say with any certainty whether they were achieving Value for Money or not.

There was access to all the BVPI's across London, which showed almost a scatter gun relationship between unit costs and performance. In general the trend was that the more one spent the better the performances, but it went much further than that.

We were concentrating on the 'Street Scene', including Highways management, wider Environmental aspects and Anti-Social Behaviour, plus the affects on Open Spaces and Housing Land. This was a massive review, with far reaching affects on both the community, and the council. The budgets involved were around £35M per annum, so understanding the issues was essential.

We dealt with 'compare' from two totally different standpoints: The first was from the broad council budgets, we sent out enquiries to several other similar boroughs, with a particular focus on those ones which were perceived as being effective for some of the issues being dealt with.

We provided a template for the areas we were looking at, and asked for data for previous and last years' expenditure / income, plus this years' budget. We had committed to share our findings with all of them, and volunteered to be the hosts for a bi-annual benchmarking club. There were lots of agreements, with many accountants saying it was a great idea.

We got a dribble of responses, and little buy in. So we tried to be more positive, an accountant did the rounds, collecting data on a live basis as he visited our neighbours. We had far more data, but aligning and comparing it, was dreadfully awkward. At this stage we also used director-level networks to drum up involvement and commitment.

We called the first meeting with the intention of getting accountants, and an operational officer from each borough around the table, to see what we could learn and identify where data needed to be cleaned up as we were not comparing apples with apples. Only one operational officer arrived, thankfully from our own borough, and while most boroughs were represented, several junior officers substituted at the 11th hour had no ownership of their data, and little interest in the process.

To cut a long story short, we gradually generated more interest, and through that, better information. Operational contacts were made, and some of the startling budget differences were reduced. For instance, where we were collecting budgets on refuse collection, one account included refuse disposal, apparently more than doubling their unit costs for collection. We added in some data from Cipfa returns re waste, population, households, lengths of streets etc. to start the process of calculating the cost per activity.

This also showed that some of the BVPI's across London, which had been audited for years, could not possibly be correct, ie. Cost of refuse collection per household, should be in simple terms, costs divided by households, equals cost per household. The sums sang out errors in some places, and caused a little interest when these boroughs were asked whether they were aware of the anomalies. The famous 'league tables' proved a little unreliable. At least in football you know how many games are won and drawn, even if goals are incorrectly disallowed.

We also started in the opposite direction, initially there was a 'quick and dirty exercise' to analyse our own data in a series of innovative ways, trying to show to all that they had good data, if only they would actively use it.

We then sought meaningful detailed benchmarking data for an array of SoR type activities, and found nothing of sufficient use across London, so had to go further a field. We used the PSnet service for refuse collection, street sweeping, recycling and highways maintenance. While this was an invaluable source of information, it contained a massive range of council data, from the smallest rural DC's to the largest Metropolitans. That would need further work.

Getting our own data was an exercise on its own, this was harder than when you have your own DSO, as there were a range of contractors involved, not all of whom were too motivated to show their internal financial structures. Where some were to say a little reluctant to give information, we conducted interviews to get as much information as possible, and then interpolated the rest.

This suddenly started to produce a few significant variations, why was say, litter picking per 100m so much dearer at this borough than the average, and yet a neighbouring borough was more than twice that cost?

To try to get a truer 'like for like' comparator we spent a whole day with the benchmarking expert at PSnet, who would not release specific data on any one contributor, but was able to focus on the anomalies, the data that flew off the paper, and said look at me, I'm different. We started to learn through knowledge, rather than beliefs, and through that learning do something about our own situation.

Bringing all the information together, and producing a meaningful Board report was no mean feat, but we did, and it did lead to a very interesting debate. The drafting process was also an invaluable learning process. Suddenly there was a committed buy in from some very senior officers, who had taken little interest in the 'Compare' process. Their services were going to be paraded to the chief executive and members, in a degree of clarity unheard of, warts and all.

There were some misinterpretations in data even at that late point, previous decisions and policies emerged, which had clouded why certain costs were so high. Some budgets were set for 'X', but used for 'Y', and it would be problematic to expose this. Thus there were two levels of refining the data in the report, to enable meaningful debate, and not to cause an open warfare.

It became clear that within that debate that there were still areas to probe, and places to learn more about. But, virtually for the first time there were meaningful details, ideas and concepts to probe; these enabled informed decision making, and created the first BV review at that borough which had genuinely probed the thornier aspects of Value for Money.

Challenge

The question of *Challenge* within a BV Review creates a whole series of tensions, with stresses, accusations and resentment all possible outcomes. One of the recurring themes as an interim manager in a BV Review, is to act as an internal challenger. To someone like me, challenging the whys and wherefores of an organisation and being paid for the privilege is brilliant, 'Thank you Best Value!'

But being the challenger for four to nine months is a risky business. Its really a question of balance, to go in and simply say, here are all the things you are doing wrong, put them right creates only negative energy, focuses too much on dispiriting everyone, and the access to get to more information suddenly becomes an impossibility.

Even being aware of these issues, it has proven impossible for me to keep on that narrow path of finding the brilliant, and praising it, finding the nearly good and tweaking it to get better, and then identify the areas that really don't work at all.

In the inner London borough they established a group called the 'Challenge Partners' who met once a month, and, thankfully, there were a couple of very vociferous partners who had much more stinging stories than some of mine. So I certainly wasn't a lone wolf. But I was the only person digging inside the organisation on a daily basis. As

I got in deeper, there were at least four groups of people with their own motivators: My sponsor urged me virtually every week to get in there and really upset the applecart, challenge 'unmercifully', make them squirm... The management team were cautiously thankful that so many aspects were good, and concerned about the not so goods, The managers directly involved with the services, grew increasingly defensive as the review went on and some performance management people became openly hostile until after the waste inspection.

In fact the waste inspection was both a saviour and a barrier. It was fast-tracking this pre inspection process, that suddenly turned me from a long term threat and enemy in some peoples eyes, to their greatest ally. I had to be focussed on promoting the positive, to align all the good stuff, and improve the bad stuff. I was very pleased after the inspection was over for one of the people who had moved to apparently hate me, to come over, apologise for his behaviour, and shake me by the hand. All he had ever heard was the negative, and missed the balancing positive that I had previously tried to espouse.

The small DC was in most ways the most receptive to challenge. A Yorkshire friend had briefed me before starting this assignment regarding the ethos there: *look them in the eyes, and tell it as it is!* An interesting plan for dealing with councillors – don't butter them up, be direct, honest, and bold. This was certainly a new method for me, but worth a try.

We did a huge amount there in a very short time. Even the committee chairman cringed when I briefed the full council that success could only be achieved if they all signed up to the changes, and publicly supported the changes, even through the tough times. I had just given a 'warts and all' presentation on all the complaints that a kerbside wheeled bin scheme, with twin boxes would create. How many losers there would be, and how volatile the opposition would be. It was a hung council with an election seven months away. They were brilliant, with one slight slide from one member, who was soundly rounded on, and then withdrew his comments openly.

Needless to say if the balance of challenge is overplayed, your employers can soak up so much, and no more. If you want continuity of employment, not all places are as tolerant as that Northern DC.

Consult

Consult has become increasingly difficult in many ways. The British public has suffered 'over consultation' for a fair while, and as a nation we are incredibly tolerant, (or apathetic). In a small town of say 15,000 people there will be around 150 people that really take an interest in adding value to their environment.

Those people will make up virtually all the district and town councillors, the school governors, the scout and guide Leaders, the football managers, run a youth centre, organise the annual parade, fetes, and protest groups.

The other 14,850 may take some interest in certain things, and when the 'Not in my backyard' NIMBY aspects arise, either get a little heated, or sign a petition, but otherwise everything happens for them and their families.

So consult is difficult, who cares is the most likely response, so how can you get meaningful feedback which is balanced, representative and statistically valid?

We chipped away at this in the inner London borough, with borough wide annual surveys, triennial London wide surveys, and then a suite of specifics to the review using varying methods.

We set out some ideas to be tested, and tried to get opinions on these prior to starting some trials, then during the trials and after. We were trying to get places cleaner, and reduce the fear of crime, so we conducted surveys in streets, estates and market areas.

These were generally day time and thus didn't pick up on the night-scene, and gave an unbalanced slant. We got more females than males, and generally an older profile than average, particularly as there was a high proportion of under twenties in the borough.

We also conducted staff surveys, sought the views of the front line staff, most of whom lived in the borough, and set up internet surveys for people who lived and worked in the borough. We also set up two evening meetings to use the customer Panel, who were to be paid for attending. These were so small, and imbalanced that they just became a complaining workshop, largely nothing to do with the review. Some pro-active work was done in schools, to see how the increasing age of pupils affects their environmental objectivity. The "its cool to litter" protocol with puberty was a very strong message.

Overall we got lots of feedback, and realised that the framing of questions, and location for interviews (ie in a market, full of litter), influenced the answers. Technically the feedback was not balanced, in terms of gender, age or ethnicity, but it did all add value to the final BV Action Plan.

In other Authorities customer panels are very effective, although they can be so obvious when a 'mystery customer' exercise is launched unannounced on the service providers; after about three calls you all know it's started again.

At a housing authority which had a quite mature customer panel, a pair of consult days were organised, one a few weeks after the BV Review had started, and the second to feedback on recommendations and to test reactions.

It was really very pleasant to meet these customers; they had so many nice things to say about the team being reviewed. Out of 17 observations and complaints raised, only three were about the team in question, and the rest was an opportunity to raise issues, relating to the rest of the HA, some of which had a fair history to them.

However, even with such a small strike rate of contribution to the review area, they did add value, in that relatively unidentified issues came to light, enabling a broader brief to emerge, and some more efficiencies to be achieved.

Continuous Improvement

CI is very precious to me, in that CI was the term used by Deming to describe Kaizen or what perhaps to most people would see as, 'TQM plus a lot more!' Reading from the other end of this book, will cover CI as it should be covered.

The process of CI within BV is somewhat management by numbers, both in terms of BVPI's and Finances. The introduction of the Gershon reports on efficiencies takes up a lot of the issues on efficiencies, and will add political fuel to many debates. Councils are now required to identify how they will get 2.5% more efficient this year than last and send that data to the government. This started in April 2005 and will need to be repeated for the next two years.

The initial BV inspections led, unsurprisingly, to quite low evaluations for services and councils. A friend of mine who has risen to chief executive surmised that if the Auditors show a poor base, its far easier to gradually improve outcomes, and as a result prove that Best Value was the right approach! There must be more than a grain of truth to that view.

What also was interesting was the stated ambitions of Best Value, there would be a string of BVPI's designed to enable comparisons, and to give a constant stretch target for all to aspire to. After the first year these were published, and the target to achieve, was that upper quartile (UQ) position, which had to be equalled or surpassed over the next five years.

Of course there needed to be a 'bedding in' period, and a great many clarifications were asked for, many of them were in turn addressed. In the environmental / waste area, there were sets of data inter-dependant on each other. These included, with slight simplifications:

- Kg of waste per head of population
- Percentage waste diverted
  – Recycling – Composted – Energy from waste
- Missed collections per 100,000 collections made
- Cost of collection per household
- Cost of disposal per household

The target was to achieve upper quartile in every one of these! If an authority made collections in sacks from the edge of property, but didn't supply the sacks to the customers, took the materials to a local incinerator, and it covered a fairly small district then their costs per household would be very small, and waste diversion very great.

If a council had a fairly large, often congested district, used wheeled bins, collected weekly, with a compost collection plus separate recyclates, took these to a materials recycling facility, and achieved very high rates of recycling, their recycling and composting rates would be very high, and their costs would be high as well.

The first organisation above may also have very low rates of refuse per household, and the latter very high rates. These are outcomes of specification, technological and environmental advances. The decisions at each location may be right for them, but they could not hit upper quartile in all areas.

The targets for councils in this area were quite punitive, although strictly outside the rigours of Best Value. The councils which had made good early progress on recycling would have to double the percentage, while the laggards could catch up with the position where the others had been. These targets for additional waste diversion were not allowed for in the BV upper quartile targets for finances!

The other brilliant feature at first was this ability to hang on to the UQ target for a single BVPI and hit it. The amount of BVPI's that were eliminated before even the third year was startling, with many others getting redefined. A consultative exercise in the Summer of 2004 was interesting, the government (Audit Commission?) were considering streamlining and simplifying BVPI's so the above cluster would be split up into sub-categories, to have over 20 indicators instead of a handful. The concept was to streamline the BVPI's, but in fact it just created far more (that's a government reduction!) The authority said creating a far wider, differently defined set of PI's would add to the costs to monitor and produce future data, with little or no benefit to customers.

Another wonderful aspect of BVPI's is their definitions, and the ability to compare like with like. I have done battle with Defra and the Audit Commission for five of the last six years on trying to get errors addressed, and to address individual nuances. As a consultant I found it far easier to 'do battle' as I could keep the particular council I was representing out of the fray, and distance them from the argument. Via this process I have twice had Emails from the Audit Commission (BVPI Section) instructing me to 'fudge it' as there wasn't a reasonable solution.

One of these was with regard to a large borough with a PFI deal on Waste Disposal. The way in which the PI's could be interpreted took them from a laggard on one PI to best in London, and for another PI made it plummet from a good position, to one of the worst, including infringing statutory targets for recycling. When the final figures were published a few months after leaving, I was surprised to see even another interpretation had been hammered out.

In 2002 a new BVPI (199) was introduced regarding the cleanliness levels of Streets, open spaces, estates, and public areas in all sectors of the authority for litter and detritus. This had a 65 page booklet to regiment people to manage that single PI, forced frequent inspections to set parameters of various tranches of land, with an enforced feedback system to the centre for collation and monitoring.

Detritus is one aspect, where you need to assess this in parks, is detritus *at* the edge of park path, the *edge* of the path, or *material* that should be swept? Fortunately country lanes which have sheep and cattle traverse them frequently don't seem to be included.

It was altered after a short time so that instead of 4 levels of cleanliness in line with the EPA 1990, (A, B, C & D) that it would have seven levels, so that borderline issues could be taken on board. By April 2005 this single BVPI has been increased to 4 BVPI's so that Graffiti, Fly-posting and Fly-tipping can be included.

This happened after a government decision was taken to 'Streamline' BVPI's. The term streamline in the Dictionary says, "Simplify, make more efficient or better organised". This was part of a process to take five BVPI's and make them into fifteen.

So, returning to Continuous Improvement, how can a single set of definitions be set for inner London and the deepest countryside and be equitably compared? In general, they can not!

How can financial implications be set for the whole nation, when there are significant variables of circumstances not least of which are the population density/sparcity factors?

Now look at the arbitrary setting of targets, such as from Gershon. I worked for an absolutely brilliant Finance Director some years ago, who sadly died of cancer after a few years as chief executive. I learned a great deal from him, and he a little from me.

One of his strengths was in long term planning, and ensuring meaningful Business Planning by every Division and Section of the council. He tried long and hard to bring in a 3% financial efficiency gain from every section, every year, so that finances could be created for service improvements, and the dreaded 'initiatives'.

I tried hard to convince him it wasn't such a good, or easy idea, particularly if the bulk of the spend is say for a third party contractor to perform a growing service (say due to increased population), against a traditional long term contract. This he conceded was an exception.

I then showed him that within my DSO we had reduced our unit recharges by 14% in two areas over the previous 18 months. If I were charged with achieving 3% this year, next year, etc. I would be tempted to hold back any savings through innovation so that I had capacity in the bank for next year. They were interesting times, I didn't have to make 3% in each area, but was encouraged to keep adding value.

If the government arbitrarily enforce a 2.5% annual saving on all, doesn't that make life proportionally easier for the cash rich, and virtually impossible for the impoverished? It's the same as I was postulating earlier, forcing all to 'do CCT' was a mistake, it flooded the market, caused too many mistakes, and added to the costs of the better organisations. If all have to get 2.5 percent cheaper, not better, not more efficient, how will that affect services in Authorities that physically can't deal with that pressure?

As far as the biggest issues are concerned, there is no way I could give the answers to achieving fair funding for local government, although I am very tempted to suggest that each council should be fully funded from its local populace and businesses. Then there would be clarity as to the cost effectiveness per council, and where the real problem areas are. That is then greatly influenced by the ratio of working public; areas where there is full employment will have a high proportion of people to pay taxes, and a good level of businesses to pay their rates.

In more impoverished areas, there will be low employment, low pay and relatively few businesses. Thus you could get the rich getting richer, and the poor getting poorer, which proves there are no simple answers.

Total local funding would also create far more interest in local democracy, as your vote would directly impact on your pocket. It should also greatly reduce the tensions between central and local government, and dare I say it, reduce other forms of taxation.

Performance Management

Performance management (PMgt.) is one of the best aspects of BV, and is far too lightly addressed in too many places; again, this will feature strongly at the other end of this book.

Many places have PM officers sat near the centre of each department, or at the centre of the council. These officers tell people what they need to have, harvest data from all the other sections, castigating anyone that is late, or who have submitted defective formats.

They then produce a series of reports, showing achievements, targets, slippages and the occasional rising stars, often giving a narrative to explain why there are minor deviations from month to month, or quarter to quarter. The reports are, of course, all looking backwards. Well you would expect them to be! I once described this version of PMgt. as being like driving down the M1 by looking in the rear view mirror, a perfect view of where you have been, but no idea of where you are going, or what's ahead. Does that have enough impact for you?

Deming was a great advocate of understanding your business, and not meddling with it. He devised a very simple practicable analogy to detecting failures in a business and reporting on changes from month to month, called the red bead test. This had a number of red beads (failures) and about 4 times that number of white beads (successes).

Over a long period of time you will have a 20% failure rate, but look at each sample and you can see any number of patterns arising. It's a process in statistical control, but to our performance officers, some people are failing, and they must be identified. Please read the section on Continuous Improvement at the other end of this book.

5: Was it right to move to Best Value in the noughties?

CHAPTER SIX:
Now we have Best Value, should we keep it?

Best Value has a great many virtues, and thus it makes eminent sense to retain it, with of course a number of areas to help move it forward. Perhaps the greatest aspects to address are to discover what is best to focus on, and where?

After-all wasn't that at the heart of the philosophy, to look at the whole area of service provision at least once every five years and then act on what you find?

BV fortunately, or otherwise, is part of a wider whole, with the affects of many legislative parameters from Britain and Europe impacting on what needs to be done. It would not be politic to suggest that government should step back and work out how all the competing forces are working, seek some form of hierarchy for a Strategic Vision over say the next ten years, then start progressing in partnership.

I have kept the thrust of this on local government, and around direct services, but messages abound from other areas where playing the BV games, is indeed playing with peoples lives. In the Health Service we hear stories of ambulances averaging less than eight minutes to get a patient to a hospital and then staying outside for hours with the patient in the ambulance, while the A&E department reduces its backlog.

One of the worst of recent cases had several ambulances tied up in this way, and a person who desperately needed an ambulance, died because they could not be moved. This shows a focus on management by numbers, rather than performance management? (The work done by ambulance drivers, paramedics, doctors and nurses is truly valued. They do great work, but are then forced into ridiculous gambits by number crunching idiots following arbitrary targets.)

On a weekly basis we have heard of the deplorable state of hospital wards. These seemed to have got worse from the moment that the all powerful Matrons, lost their powers. Certainly an issue adversely affected by CCT, with few beacons of excellence to shine forth for a better tomorrow.

I was privileged to listen to Myron Tribus at the Deming Forum giving a talk on Florence Nightingale, covering what she achieved in the Crimea, and how she made a step change improvement in hospital care and cleanliness, with a phenomenal affect on the mortality rates. It would appear we need a new example to lead us away from where we are going.

In a sense it is sad that the term continuous improvement has been used in best value as it has. Both BV & CI will be tarnished for the future, making the next phase much more problematic.

But what will that next phase look like. The naming of this will, as ever, become highly political, with the election prepartions for May 2005, it was clear that BV would change. If a Labour government was returned again, BV would most likely be slightly re-invented, much the same as any high street product, n*ewer, shinier vastly improved* We no more believe most of the TV hype than politicians or estate agents.

If there had been a Conservative government, could they possibly retain something as flawed as best value? So did they have their own well thought out product to replace it?

The reality of a third term with New Labour has been a toughening up of the CPA process, diverting ever more people from doing a good job, to producing a 25 page self analysis ticking all the right boxes.

So, how do we focus on the what & where that needs to be done, how do we get to that inner sanctum of divine awareness, ensuring that we only do what is needed, in the most powerful way possible, for the greatest benefit of local.goverment.uk ?

In years gone by we had local democracy, with councillors elected against local mandates, and then getting on and doing the will of the people. It kind of works, particularly where there aren't too many pressures. Wasn't that how the infrastructure of gas, electricity, roads, and schools got built over a hundred years ago?

The work done within benchmarking, where it is done properly, shows how much power can be obtained from that process. Is it possible that a Value for Money evaluation for services at a fairly high level could be conducted, which is appreciative of local circumstances; for instance an inner City area, with considerable deprivation, which is a laggard for recycling, but this is due to the disposal costs, thus: ... The places to make better, take action, needing real support are: ...

My criticism of CCT was that it didn't go into local government as a whole, only the prescribed areas creating a paradox, but it also forced changes that were not needed in some places. [Organisations that were effective and cost effective still had to go through the process, perhaps to the detriment of costs and services] The problem was 'one size fits all.'

Best Value is potentially better than that, as it affects all of local government, but again has this issue of one size fits all. That is not a sane approach to such diverse enterprises as local government, is it?

I would suggest that a more mature attitude for the government would be to seek to use the best of BV, and consult with some of the leading lights, and laggards within LG to see where the greatest benefits can arise from the least amount of effort. This would look like a form of cost benefit analysis. The paretto analysis analogy is correct here. By addressing the 20% least effective areas, there could be an 80% gain in effectiveness. Conversely by not addressing the other 80% with arbitrary inspection, systems and mandates, they also can save the bureaucratic costs that BV imposes.

One of the powers of using information and statistics correctly together, is that clarity of vision improves. The 80/20 rule from Pareto shows that eighty percent of problems are usually caused by twenty percent of the issues. Using a simple bar chart the prime causes can be isolated and then focussed on for action. This has been applied successfully in many areas within LG and it works.

I was explaining this to a HoS within a London borough when helping him re-draft his service plan. He was depressed because of an initiative overload from on high. It was the old adage too many priorities produce no priorities at all. We went through a mini-brainstorm, mind mapped the outcomes, and quickly looked at some cause and effect diagrams together with his historic performances. The whole process took the two of us about 45 minutes. At first he thought I was saying just do the biggest problems, and wring them out until they go to zero.

I suggested that he has one of his teams quickly trained so they can visualise their data, and what causes failures, and then work on the biggest issue for each team, with the HoS riding shotgun as a supporter of their work. The bits that really surprised him were, that as the biggest issue is largely overcome, the next biggest issue probably will give the most cost benefit to deal with, and that some easy wins for something else will come to light, and they add to morale, as improvement can become a way of life.

Suddenly the HoS didn't have a great long shopping list of issues to deal with, with no strategy to get started; he had some processes to break down the problems to manageable bite sizes, and an awareness of how to deal with this mass of performance management data from the department centre.

So even at the highest levels, the biggest issues can have evaluation, weighting and a structured plan to move forward. Does that sound better than a scatter gun approach that appears to be the norm from BV, legislation overloads and the annual funding debates?

Now look at the broadening issues within local government. The government are still very fond of the Regional government agenda, despite a bloody nose from the electorate in the North East where they firmly believed they would have most support.

With no elected tier at regional levels, how can the aspirations still be achieved? Clearly the answer is via non-elected methods. Regional planning, development and transport are all moving forward. Co-operating authorities are fast developing regional procurement, improvement and integration abilities. This will help challenge duplication and poor performances, but will further dilute the uniqueness of each authority, and thus the electorate will be even less interested in local politics, so the voting levels will continue to plummet.

However, with all the indications of global warming, a more local vision of sustainability is also needed.

The focus now is to get closer to neighbourhoods, probably installing parishes into London and other metropolitan authorities, enabling a defined local role for backbench councillors who were disempowered as a result of cabinet working methods.

The ideas at present are to enable small areas within an authority to have some say, with the ability to spend locally raised monies (via a precept) manage discreet resources either as a top-up to, or instead of the wider authority.

This could include areas such as street cleansing, graffiti, fly-posting, minor repairs to paths and fences, playground management/ maintenance. In the inner London authority the service delivery and management was being conducted via eight generic working teams, with a strong liaison with the community, police and various local voluntary groups.

The prospects of having top up teams to add local value to local agendas is a sound idea, but could lead to the prime contractor reducing input, and therefore increasing profits, while the local teams do more than they should.

The laws have also changed enabling 24 hour drinking, adding significant pressures to inner urban areas, where anti social behaviour is already a burden from say 9pm to around 1am. Fights, muggings, theft, noise and damage are occuring on the streets with more people ending up in hospital. The Clean Neighbourhoods and Environment Act greatly increases the powers for an authority to deal with all the above but requires even more awareness of processes and powers. Once a few revellers have had £75 fixed penalty fines for the above, perhaps a little more sobriety will occur.

Fast arriving on the horizon is the likely roll out of unitary councils, perhaps to create a greater need for regional government, while local education authorities look like disappearing to make way for more powerful school bodies. The intended move away from the CPA and JAR process in 2008, cutting out the Audit Commission while establishing local inspectorates, could be another step to strenghthen regional govermnent.

CHAPTER SEVEN:

How can Best Value become a reality?

Best Value should not only seek, but achieve what is best for customers, thus all the clever work rounds to make PI's look good at the expense of customers must be eliminated. The questions really is what is best for customers, and how do you stop foul play?

I'm not one of the 'Big Players' in local government, but I really do care about adding value. The lead member for environment at a London borough, where consultants had been a taboo, institutionally hated by members, suddenly found an interim manager who both cared, and tried to make a difference. He described me as 'Passionate about Refuse' as that was the area I was working on, and I said to him, "No, I'm not passionate about refuse, I'm passionate about excellent service delivery"

To make a positive difference people need ingredients: Knowledge, Information, Education, Statistics and so forth. Above all a methodology is needed to evaluate how all the conflicting priorities can be evaluated and merged together to produce a master plan.

The strategic direction of a local authority is of paramount importance. The chief executive, directors and lead members must be able to build a strategy, and have a constancy of purpose to see that strategy through.

I had thought about having a chapter on chief executives, and decided against it. With the mixture of permanent posts, and interim ones, I have worked with a good number of chief executives, and have seen some really good ones, and others that wouldn't know a strategy if they tripped over it.

People make a business what it is, if they have drive, energy, ambition and can communicate that coherently, they will make anything seem possible.

I was recruited to a relatively small DC, and found a management team that was so vibrant and dynamic, it was infectious. They did great things, took some risks, most of which succeeded, and that DC 'Out-punched its weight' for the Community.

It had services that were among the best in Britain, with an appreciative public, and a high profile public perception. It gained many grants from various places, and added value to the infrastructure. Two years after I started there, the chief executive was promoted to a bigger, more prestigious authority, and a more 'conservative' chief was taken on.

Gradually all the fire and fun went out of the leadership, the better people moved on, and the DC became what it always could have been, a small DC in proportion to its neighbours. Where the previous Chief had taken some risks, and they hadn't quite worked out, he was blamed with their 'failures'. I left!

As an interim I have been heartened by many chief executives; they really do care about their organisations, they evaluate information, and take decisions on that information. Most understand delegation, as it is impossible to head a large organisation properly, without letting go of the areas of specialism, and fun areas of work, that helped to get them there.

For directors and senior officers to get freedoms to manage, they need to prove that they have a right to those freedoms, and can honour the contract that letting go by the Chief creates.

Best Value must be a strategic part of direction and management, and not a tack on to the day job. Performance management can not be a centralist monthly role, simply harvesting data, and presenting it in a 'supposedly learned way' to the executive.

Every organisation that I have worked for in the last thirteen years has had good information systems and has got a degree of pollution in that information, causing them to get reporting wrong, and to work on the wrong issues.

There is a better way! Gershon has the right threads of thought about saving money, but this simply has not been integrated into a methodology that enables greater efficiency, less costs, and most importantly of all, achieving Performance management rather than Managing the PI's.

For BV to be exactly that, Best Value, we must stop tampering with perfectly good, or adequate areas of service delivery, and focus our efforts on the 20% of issues that cause 80% of the problems.

We must also focus on the most costly areas, and seek to either reduce the costs, or create a new Value for Money. What BV is getting increasingly wrong is the focus on league tables. However the rankings and comparisons continue, and will encourage and cause an industry of 'doing the wrong things better'.

CHAPTER EIGHT:

Managing in Best Value

Best Value should be an enabler, not another millstone. The London borough in chapter 1 sought to make best use of the positives, so that's probably the message, seek the positive! The processes should always be to seek 'adding value'. Challenging what you do and why, challenge methods, systems, controls and constraints, and don't hang on to ideas because of sentiment.

Following a marathon chapter 5, the last two chapters are deliberately short:

Should we keep Best Value? Yes!

How to make Best Value become a reality? Integrate it into the core of everything you do, and don't let anyone fudge the records at the expense of the public.

So how should anyone work to 'Manage in Best Value?' An associate and friend, John Seddon, is one of the most eminent thinkers about Continuous Improvement in the Country. He and his Company, have added value to countless businesses, housing associations, and yes, the Public Sector.

John is passionate about quality and efficiency. He has pet hates, inappropriate government Targets being one of them. Another is ISO 9001, John believes that ISO 9001 must be abolished, and that it does far more harm than good, and in many ways I agree, but not totally.

Achieving ISO 9001 is a tough task; it takes energy, time and resources. Despite the fact that ISO 9001 is called 'Quality Assurance' it neither adds Quality, nor assures that Quality will be added. Admittedly the new brand ISO 9001, 2000 is better than its former brand, which may have been better than BS 5750 before that.

Now to the 'Millstone effect':

Many councils have their suite of initiatives, they are rolled out in a launch of publicity, there is a 'thou must' directive for integration into business plans (service plans) and your way of working. After a few questions and grumbles, people go away with a grudging agreement to comply. If the authority is really committed it will have a champion, or champions to force feed the message.

Some HoS will go away and dutifully comply, place it in the business plan, and some will even act on it straight away and do something about it, perhaps.

A fairly large DC used to love its initiatives and rolled them out all the time to their heads of service. Initiative overload and death by a thousand initiatives was the general second tier banter. In addition as head of the DSO, I had the wonderful inheritance that comes from winning large contracts for the next seven years.

In one we had to achieve ISO 9001 (quality assurance), and in another we had to achieve ISO 14001 (Environmental management). In the meanwhile the DC decided that it needed Investors in People (IiP). So to some extent that was the full house! The concept behind specifying ISO 9001 was that the council could learn from this, and see if they wanted to do it too. The person who drafted that took no further interest in the matter, nor did any client officers, other than to address financial penalties if we were late in achievement.

The DSO had been working on continuous improvement for several years, and had one of the best set of PI's in the country, achieving less than 15 missed collections per 100,000, excellent customer satisfaction, and had moved from 4% to 15% recycling in a matter of months. The housing maintenance side was improving quickly as well, and would have been upper quartile had BV existed then.

But we had to do ISO 9001! We looked long and hard at it, the two most senior officers went off and studied to near black belt at evening classes and then we chose our certification partner. It was tough going, hard work, we had to get a practitioner on board to help us with the translation from local government to ISO, but we gradually got there and got the tick in the box. BUT, we did something different with this. We put it in the *core* of how we worked, and used the processes to add value to the way we worked.

Our refuse manager was brilliant at delivering a service, but not so good at keeping it within budget, so we built that as part of the ISO 9001 procedures. Suddenly we found some new level of controls and an opportunity to get even better than we were under a CI process alone. It also helped us be ahead of the game on some emerging H&S initiatives.

So when the council was going to do IIP, I got onto the centre stage to help design the IIP experience. This was partly because what works fine for head office staff, is a little strange for refuse collectors and carpenters.

We designed the how and what, and again placed this into the core of operations. The monthly management meeting had new elements regarding induction, training, and the interfaces with the business plan. Team interviews would often occur in the refuse lorries (using a captive audience principle), and some very interesting business planning sessions with the workforce never once mentioned the expression business planning.

ISO 14001 was more of struggle, but we got there, and after a while, made it self financing.

The point is, instinctively I would never opt to seek ISO 9001 voluntarily, but we had to, and we made it add value. The amount of time effort and resource needed for the achievement would have been far better invested in working on continuous improvement. Thus if you want to spend say £30,000 on improving your service, don't chose ISO 9001, as you probably will be disappointed. BUT, if you have to do ISO 9001 or getting back to this book, Best Value, do it properly and make it add value!

Thus the point of this very brief chapter is to make Best Value fundamental to how you, your team, and all their teams work. Of course, that can give a problem if BV is no longer the Governments aim!

I would suggest that from a political standpoint that Best Value is retained in such a way that:

- Performance management is retained as a prerequisite for all government.
- Benchmarking is a mandate to prove top 75% Value for Money
- The majority of all authorities are trusted without major audits.
- All authorities can request special audits, via the scrutiny group
- The top 50% have freedoms to deliver locally mandated services
- The third quartile have freedoms with checked planning
- The bottom 25% VfM group are forced to improve value for money
- Any authority found to gerrymander figures or act against the interest of customers' moves to the 4th quartile for a year.

This ends Politics or Quality and has given a brief view of the affects of how government and legislation affects doing the work. Starting at the other end of this book is Quality or Politics which deals with delivering high quality services within a political world. I hope that is not too confusing!

Quality or Politics?

Achieving excellence in public service delivery

DAVE GASTER

Nisbet media

Nisbet Media Ltd

29 Mellstock Avenue

Dorchester

Dorset DT1 2BG

email: books@nisbetmedia.co.uk

First Publ.ished 2006

Designed by Julian Slade

Typeset in Warnock Pro

ISBN 0-9553000-0-2

ISBN 978-0-9553000-0-4

Published by Nisbet Media Ltd

© Dave Gaster

Printed in England

CONTENTS

Chapter	Title	Page

Foreword by Ossie Dodds,
Director of the Public Services Network

Much has been written in the last 20-30 years about local government and the changes that successive governments have imposed on it – often without real understanding of local government or without appreciating how it really works and is perceived by the public it serves/provides essential services to.

This book is different – it has been written by someone with a local government background. The author continues to work with local authorities as a consultant or interim manager and has therefore experience of a variety of shapes, sizes, political and managerial arrangements. He has also been involved with a wide variety of services and local people's reactions to them.

The book and its companion volume "Politics or Quality" draw on all of the above knowledge and experience and is a useful addition to the literature available on local government, its services and the effects of successive government attempts to improve or change things.

I encourage everyone to read it carefully – don't be put off by the title or contents list! Read it from end to end and use the messages it contains to improve your services/council's performance or to think more deeply about ideas for change and how to implement them. That is what it has been written for and if it succeeds both local government and the United Kingdom will all be better off.

Oswald A. Dodds, MBE
Director, Public Services Network

Introduction

This book focuses on the achievement of *quality* in services - mainly in Local government but also in housing associations and health authorities, addressing the impacts of central government, with a number of case studies and examples of how "Best Value" and "Continuous Improvement" can really be addressed. Against this, there is the paradox of an increasing level of re-interpretation and fine tuning by the government, and a reducing interest in Local government by the electorate.

It is imperative for businesses and government to understand the opportunities that systematic methods of working can offer. A long term commitment to continuous improvement can achieve a quantum leap in efficiency, compared with the arbitrary 2.5% per annum required in Sir Peter Gershon's review of public sector efficiency .

I've tried to offer practical, graphic examples of how continuous improvement can be achieved. There is no single way of doing things. Nor should you ever use a tool kit approach. If someone comes to your door and has a ready made solution to your problems, how can they possibly know whether it will fit, or do irreparable harm?

Continuous improvement provides a way to address how your organisation actually works. It will help you improve what is done, eliminate mistakes, and reduce the costs of doing things wrong. The Japanese use the term Kaizen, where all the people in an organisation are working to improve the way it works.

Examples are mainly from areas such as refuse collection and housing maintenance, including the administration and financial areas that directly support them. These should enable readers to bridge the gap from these services to their own, as I had to bridge the gap with examples from the motor industry some thirteen years ago. In

addition I have focussed on several areas within offices such as invoice processing to help create new linkages and thought processes.

There are many graphs and tables of data, together with ideas of how to do things in less complicated ways.

Could it be possible for two people to brainstorm a business plan, draft a mind map of it, deal with cause and effect, and then start on an action plan in 45 minutes? Well it's highly unusual, and fairly sketchy, but it can take a de-motivated officer into a more positive frame of mind when dealing with a plethora of corporate initiatives as well as the day job.

This book looks at good practice, and lessons to be learned, often drawing on sporting and other analogies.

Now for the unusual part: It is in fact, two books, starting at this end Quality or Politics, but starting at the other end it's Politics or Quality.

Quality or Politics is focussed on the mechanism of continuous improvement, best practice, and how to positively re-invent an organisation. Politics or Quality is focussed on legislation, compulsory competitive tendering and best value.

I hope that you find both views useful, both now and in the future.

Dave Gaster

Director, Support Services Direct

Why Quality or Politics?

There is still hope that Quality and Politics will co-exist. The past 25 years have been a golden age for local government, if not in terms of the number of out-standing achievements, then by the fact that a deluge of change has been more than coped with.

In the best run authorities there is a wealth of examples of outstanding leadership, with excellent service delivery in terms of customer satisfaction and Value for Money (VfM). Even in some which don't have outstanding leadership there are enclaves of brilliance, which do well in spite of the odds against them.

Local government is a poorly understood environment. A week ago I listened to a senior civil servant saying local government had a much greater wealth of competent managers who cope with major changes, and lamenting the inability of the civil service to voluntarily achieve a small fraction of similar savings.

Yesterday I was talking to a senior manager from a blue chip company who was lambasting his local authority, and expounding on the difficulties he had lobbying senior officials in the Department for Agriculture and Rural Affairs, Defra. His view was that local authorities were poor, and the civil service quite good, but slow at doing anything positive. After discussion he started to understand the significant demands and constraints on LAs and how frequently Defra and most other government departments re-invent legislation to make it that bit harder to really work.

This book will focus on why good quality exists, how best to achieve real quality, and what the characteristics are which make it easier to achieve. The other book deals with the more Political aspects.

In the following chapters there is a mixture of theory, practice and examples. In an attempt to maintain clarity, I have listed all

abbreviations and acronyms on pages 96-98, and explained their meaning when first used. Now, some questions for you to ponder:

Service delivery officers, have you ever had:

• All refuse collected for three weeks with no missed collections at all (300,000 collections)?

• Not one single Emergency, Urgent or Routine Housing Maintenance job late in a month?

• Not one late void in a month, and an average re-let period of 2.6 weeks for the whole year?

• Upper quartile BVPI's for all your services?

• All invoices paid on time?

• Far more compliments coming in from customers than complaints?

• Reduced tyre costs by 60%?

• Genuine partnering with sub-contractors and suppliers?

In four different authorities this has been either achieved, or moved substantively to this position.

Financial officers, have you done this, or would like to:

• Paid all invoices on time?

• Reduce unit costs by an average of 14%?

• Eliminated duplications, paperwork, and processes to make admin 4 times more efficient?

• Had the ability for meaningful overnight financial reporting Emailed to your desk every day?

• Eliminated the need for a call handling centre, because there are no complaints?

• See the real costs of supplies and services reduce five years in a row?

Personnel Officers, are you used to:

• All levels of a service unit actively engaged in building the service plan?

- The management team having good personnel information actively used at least every month?
- Induction pro-actively managed and monitored?
- Quarterly (or bi-annual) interviews with all staff, fully recorded (with both parties well motivated)?
- Risk management working properly for H&S, harassment, equal opportunities?
- Long term planning to ensure continuity of employment levels?

The capabilities of CI are phenomenal, but it does take a different mind set, and there will be challenging decisions on the way. There are two almost conflicting requirements: "You must never walk past a problem that should be resolved", and "You must never meddle". These two together are tricky as meddling can include jumping to a conclusion.

The functions of management will also change. You need a 'Constancy of purpose', to avoid swinging from priority to priority. You should make it easier for your staff to do their work, removing the barriers that are not needed. CI is about working smarter, not harder.

Then you will confront Corporate issues. Many authorities set arbitrary targets, based on trends, historic blips or the elusive upper quartile imperative. I devote most of a chapter to this, as unless the chief executive is on board with Continuous Improvement, as described here, there could be conflict.

Arbitrary targets are to some extent meddling. If you haven't got the correct and abundant information to know where your organisation is inefficient, how can you move it forward? If there are a plethora of new controls being introduced from Personnel or Finance, does anyone ever model the impact these may have on corporate effectiveness? What about the impacts these have on service delivery?

Within many outward facing units, the changes of legislation have significant affects on effectiveness and costs. These are at least three fold; Monitoring legislation and being ready for it, Managing the Change Process to the new system, including bedding it in to a new routine, and lastly the actual affects of doing things differently, whether that be more processes, more inspections or more physical

works. (Rarely, if ever, does new legislation make it easier to do work)

As a last area within an introduction scenario many fast moving organisations have a fair degree of 'Fire Fighting' within middle and senior management levels. CI has a tendency to bring order and control. It's usually hard work but as time goes on, things get easier. For many that is a blessing. Stress reduces, productivity increases, and there is an opportunity for more fun at work. However, for those rare people who love 'Fire Fighting', CI can be a problem. Throughout the process, keep those people in mind. Consider, even if you are one of them?

CHAPTER TWO:

Deming – The statistical approach?

W. Edwards Deming was probably the greatest contributor in the world to modern management techniques and at the forefront of quality development in Japan in the 1950's which eventually moved into America in 1960's and into Europe in the 70's and 80's. He was active right up to his 93rd year, writing books, and running his famous 4 day workshops.

I was privileged to attend two conferences with Dr. Deming in attendance in the early 90's, even having a short conversation with him. There is still a very strong pursuit of his beliefs and teachings, via the Deming Forum in the UK, with variants in most industrial countries.

Deming was a statistician by training, with a number of high level achievements within US government Departments in the mid to late 40's. In 1950, he went to Japan with other American business men to help take the Japanese industrial position out of the post war crisis.

Within months Deming was seen as being someone to listen to and respect in Japan where he didn't only make a difference, but took Japan from being an also ran, to being one of the most important industrial nations in the world.

In the 60's they greatly increased their productivity, with for instance cheap plastic toys being one of the most obvious imports into the UK. Then it was cars, initially not designed very well for the European Market, as they were small and tended to rust (as they don't use road salt in Japan, the high salt content starts steel rusting). But within a relatively short time they went from 'rust buckets' to market leaders.

Later there were many claims that it was impossible to build ships for the prices they charged, so they must be government subsidised. It was not! Japan now is a leading player for technology and manufacturing and has exported its prowess to the Pacific Ring,

the US and the UK. Look at Formula One Racing for instance, the top vehicle manufacturers are there with Toyota and Honda fast improving on their positions, with Suzuki, Hyundai, and Mitsubishi all being among the best in their fields for other motor sports.

It's not by chance that the most efficient, reliable road going cars in the world are dominated by Japan and the Asia Pacific ring. Toyota and Nissan will take most of the top ten positions for reliability. But it goes further, in the luxury car end of the Market you could compare Lexus with the top of range quality German cars. They both make similar cars with the Lexus being a great deal cheaper and more reliable.

The reason the Lexus is so much cheaper is because the way it is built. It takes less 'man hours' to build a Lexus than it takes to do the post inspection and rectification of faults for the German car. I note within my son's business study text book that it deals with Kaizen, ('every person within the organisation working towards improving the way they work', (Continuous Improvement)), and links it to Benchmarking.

Apparently the Nissan Micra faults in 1992 were measured in thousand faults per million parts. In 1993 that had reduced to 815 faults per million parts, and by 1995 reduced further to 75 per million. During that time the output per person doubled.

Consider the Japanese train service, to get from one place in Japan to another is simple. The instructions would be: Get on train on Platform 3 at 9.46, get off at 10.47 and go to platform 1. Get on train at 10.56 and get off at 11.29. Go to platform 2 and get on train at 11.44, get off train in Tokyo at 12.45.

In Britain I would be nervous where this could get me, as hospital would be a real option, as the definition of 'on time' will often make the train be moving at over 60 mph when it should be in a station.

So why is Japan so different, is it just their Culture, or can this be done anywhere? If you have a complex computer built in Japan, and a transformer/plug and lead made in China, which would you expect to cause most system failures?

The answer is that Japan isn't 'so different' they are using methods and information well, and have matured systems to such a point that reliability is the norm.

I was working at a housing association recently which had very good performances but not very good systems. Without any references to Deming I helped them with a few basic ideas. First I used their computer system to give a daily report in a meaningful way, and then I told them how to use that information to manage performance.

They were running Housing Maintenance emergency and routine work at about 98% jobs on time, and routine jobs at around 90% on time. Within two months they managed to get all work on time for the first time ever.

When I started to review their historic causes of defects, I found the biggest error was caused by the default system within the computer. If someone forgot to override the date, it would select next Sunday, why I don't know! So nine out of ten 'late' jobs were actually on time in reality. This had happened for years undetected. If nothing else it proves you should always investigate causes of error. This will be dealt with in detail later.

"Continuous Improvement is not about Tool kits"

Many learned people in the management world introduce a host of tool kits, so that you can learn five tools per night. Deming's vision of CI is nothing like that. He worked towards "A System of Profound Knowledge" where there was a very specific blend of statistical approaches, and a very high level of people issues, producing intrinsic motivation, enabling joy in work and driving fear out of the workplace.

There should be a Leadership to help people to do better, where organisations work together to improve the way they work, not competing with each other for the best short term gain. There will be no arbitrary targets, numerical goals, nor judgement on success or failure daily.

Workflows are integrated such that every part compliments every other part which re-enforces the positive actions and builds upon them.

The organisation will understand statistics, and the meaning of information particularly understanding the differences between common cause variation as opposed to special cause variation.

When I started using Deming's techniques, my approach was very mechanistic, the tool box approach, and all the people around me would know that I was trying Deming again. At that time I saw one brilliant summary sheet giving a summary of many aspects of Deming's approaches, and added to it a sheet called 'People in Continuous Improvement'. Those two documents probably scared off more potential Clients than anything else I have ever done.

We have to start somewhere with the detail of Deming's approach, and thus to me the PDCA cycle is one of the most potent. PDCA stands for Plan, Do, Check, Act. It will always be represented as shown below:

Plan is the process prior to trying out a new idea, see what you have got, analyse the data, performances, way work is done now, flow chart the long term trends, see what variation there is in the systems. Carry out work flow analysis, build cause and effect charts. Know what you are doing. Work out what you are going to try to change.

Do is a stage where, if possible, you try out a prototype of the new solution, so that you can see how it works out, before committing to a far bigger change.

Check is then quite simple, if you start a prototype trial, check the process of seeing if what you wanted to achieve, is actually happening. During this stage you will collect data, and can make slight alterations to processes, although if you do this, note them on any run charts as they may show as a special cause variation.

Act is then learning from the Check stage, the intention of the prototype was to reduce the error rate in a process, and thus make it more efficient. Did it do it? If YES, go on and actually do what you've been trying. If not, why not? If it got more efficient, but you now have seen an even bigger opportunity, should you try that out as well, if so go to Plan.

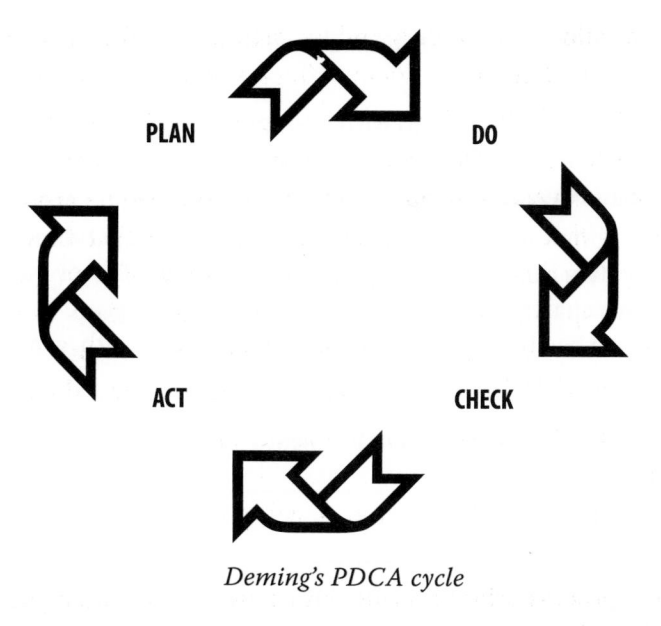

Deming's PDCA cycle

During the introduction to PDCA I have brought in references to a number of other parts of CI, some of which you may be familiar with, others will be totally new. For consultants and interim managers dealing with PDCA, there is a growing protocol to start with 'Check'. There are number of reasons for this, one of which is the initial briefing and induction by a client has assumptions and thinking based on 'Command and Control' ideas, where they believe things go wrong more often due to people than due to their systems of work.

Most Clients also want to see immediate results from an interception by a consultant, and thus they will get nervous about weeks of fact finding and little apparent action. Thus a relatively compact operation could be started on, with a checking process of data, systems, work flows and constraints. During this process there should be a strong emphasis on finding out what the real ethos of the organisation is. There are many 'no go' areas, and many strongly held principals that initial briefings will never uncover.

Using existing data and analysing it in a number of ways, can add value to the client prior to starting any change processes. Simply analysing the performance Iindicators's (PI's) for failures, causes of

failures and failure trends may enable step improvement simply by being aware of cause.

The statistical methods follow, with a couple of graphical charts taken from a real example where the Deming principals were introduced becoming increasingly powerful in their outcomes as time went on.

One of the simplest charts to use is the run chart, dependant on the volumes of data this could be run daily, weekly, monthly or quarterly. The next two charts are from a district council (DC) refuse collection service which had been in serious difficulties in 1995, with an absolute 'meltdown' of service delivery.

Refuse Missed Collections per Month – Run Chart

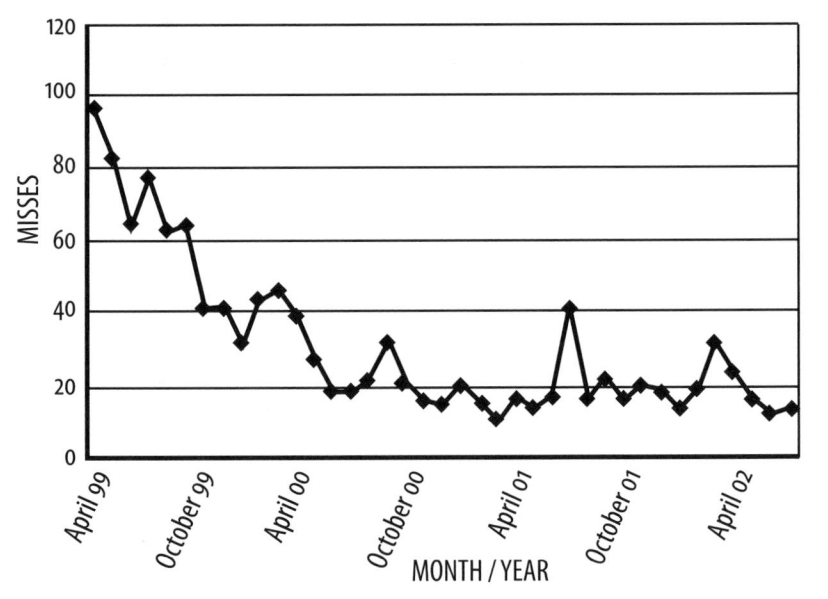

Continuous Improvement was used prior to April 1999 enabling a move from several hundred misses per month. This graph shows a number of interesting characteristics after the first stages of improvement. From April 1999 until May 2000 there is no doubt that the service delivery quality is improving.

The error rates reduce from just under 100 missed collections per month to under 20 missed collections per month. This is a five fold

improvement in quality in just over a year. The next graph will show a slightly different approach to the same data, depicting it quarterly, and adding in the average weight of waste collected per household.

The importance of understanding data is very significant; I call the above chart a 'Run chart', as it shows a constant amount of information over a period of time. An automatic option on Excel graphs is to add a trend line; sometimes these can help, other times they add to confusion.

A single trend line for the above data is not as helpful as adding a median plus upper and lower control limits. Effectively this would be done in two stages, April 99 to May 00 and then May 00 to June 02. This would then highlight the fact that there is a series of improvements initially and then a period where the work is in statistical control. Statistical Process Control is definitely an area of learning for people who try to describe the variation within data that is in statistical control, by any number of justifications.

Let me give an example of how a performance manager may (totally incorrectly) describe events from February 2000 until June 2001, (If this is too technical skip forward, but this DOES happen).

Abstracts from Management Team reports; Refuse Collection missed collections:

February 2000, Not unsurprisingly after significant improvements from April until January the performances have got worse again, rising from the unsustainable level of 31 in December through to 43 in January and now 46 in February. This is far better than the target, of 60 per month, and should still be seen as a good result. The severe winter frosts made some collections unsafe, and the short periods of daylight made spotting some bins quite difficult…

April 2000, after the slight blip in February there were 27 missed collections in April, this is the best result ever, and thus unlikely to be sustained. As we thought the better weather and longer day light hours have helped this exceptional position. We are well under this year's target of 45 missed collections per month, and should commend the refuse management for this achievement. This is an upper-quartile performance within the BVPI's set for all DC's…

August 2000, having seen such exceptional achievements for the last four months, 32 missed collections is less of a concern than the fact that a trend is emerging where missed collections are increasing at an alarming rate. They are 52% up on last month, and 78% up on May and June. I strongly recommend that immediate executive action is taken to deal with the refuse manager, who has clearly lost control of his workforce.

December 2000, the service has been performing at a very good levels for months, and 20 missed collections is below our revised target for the year of 25 missed collections per month. December is a difficult month for collections, with the bad weather and bad light, but the overall number of collections was less due to the Bank Holiday slippages over Christmas and the New Year.

June 2001, we must get increasingly concerned about this sort of problem, 41 missed collections just takes away the customer faith in the service, and it is well above our target of 20 missed collections per month. If such an event is repeated we should seriously consider a review of the refuse management Structure...

So, how many of you have seen this sort of reaction to single events in service delivery monitoring?

The run chart should not be interpreted on an individual month by month basis, the inclusion of upper and lower control limits will show there are two distinct areas to consider from April 1999 to May 2000 the data is in not in a steady state control, as there were a number of improvement actions taking place, with a continuous improvement in the median performance. However from June 2000 onwards all months would be within the upper and lower control limits.

There was a special cause to improve service delivery, and without specific monitoring of occurrences it is not possible to say whether there was a statistical cause for the increase in February 2000, as this is may be within an expected possibility.

However, there is no special reason to get alarmed about variation from May 2000 until June 2002 except for June 2001 which would count as a *special cause variation*.

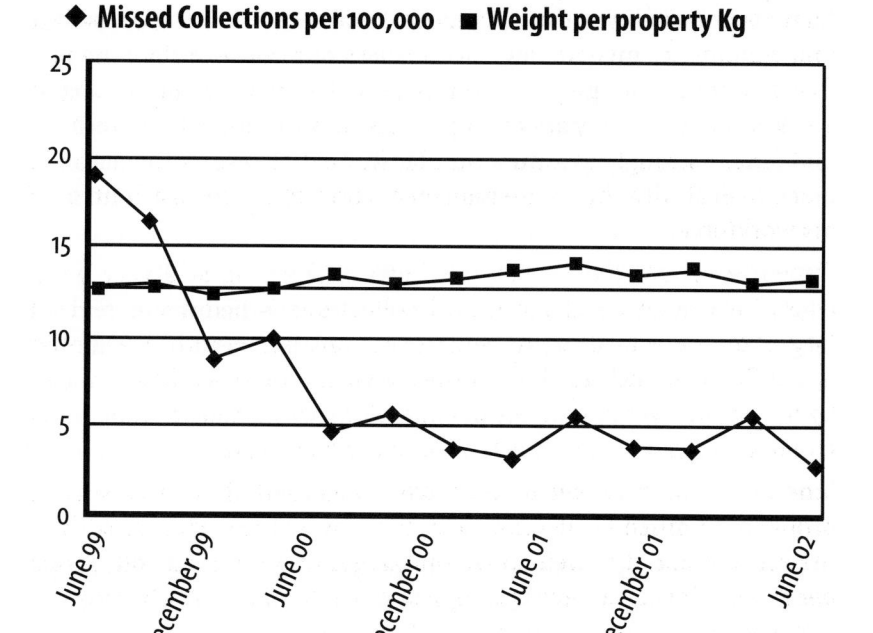

◆ **Missed Collections per 100,000** ■ **Weight per property Kg**

MONTH / YEAR

Where a run chart is kept manually, or you have the expertise to add comments to a run chart, a label should be added to the system so special causes are recorded and learned from.

In this case there was a small amount of redistribution of work between rounds, due to disproportionate increases in properties to one round. Exact lists of who does what on which day were given to drivers, plus a quick brief to loaders. But one small part of a village that should be C Round now on Tuesday was forgotten, and collected first thing the next day.

On the monthly data, which was shown first, the June information stands out as quite a spike in the otherwise stable service delivery. When the same data is analysed quarterly, as above, that spike nearly disappears. A new trend seems to arrive starting in September 2000, one month up, two months down... Yes again that is largely just common cause variation.

The common belief is that quality costs money. This example proves that quality can save money for two distinct reasons. First in an area of 360 square miles returning to a missed bin takes time, as it can add thirty miles to the distance a collection vehicle travels. Every bin not missed, saves fuel, tyre wear etc. However the missed bin scenario here went from hundreds a month, to less than twenty. There used to be a section (client) that specialised in taking calls from the public, monitoring rectification, and reporting on the contractor.

The contractor was monitoring work in exceptional detail, and the client side had little to do for Refuse, so the previous client role was incorporated into the contractor role, customers got a quicker response, service continued to improve, and a monthly audit sheet was produced for one client officer to audit, taking about ½ a day a month. The council saved in excess of £160,000 a year as a result of improved quality.

The second chart shows two sets of data, missed collections per 100,000 collections, and weight per property per collection in Kg. . Under Best Value all PI's are expected to improve. The misses per 100,000 were well into the bracket of upper quartile in 1999, and thus the improvement just moves the DC further into the super-performing range, achieving the best 2% in the country from around September 2000.

To give a 'proportionality of achievement' 25 missed collections per 100,000 was upper quartile, for this particular council; that was 25 a week. At that level there was an argument to retain a unit to monitor failures. By forcing the failure rate down, the operation costs reduced, as effectiveness increased, and then the ability to dissolve the client section emerged.

The weight per property is not so much a quality related aspect, as a specification one. To reduce the weight per property, something else needed to be done. This could include:

- Providing extra recycling facilities at the doorstep
- Increase the usage of the recycling facilities already provided
- Ensure that no one puts out side refuse and
- Instruct refuse collectors not to collect side refuse…

The data collection and monitoring table for this example is on the following pages. As this went forward it became more sophisticated, but continued to use the same chart for consistency. The BVPI auditor took less than 20 minutes to sign off the full inspection of this set of BVPI's with its supporting data, which is exceptionally fast compared to most council inspections.

There is a huge array of detailed monitoring that went behind this, and a later chapter will show a case study of how to gather data, analyse it, and then act upon it to make realistic improvements that are sustainable.

Try following the missed collections per 100,000 month by month in the above charts; it starts at around 20 and reduces sharply to around four, then after staying fairly constant for a while then starts to reduce further, to under three. For the next three years it has stayed as a world class 2.8 misses per 100,000 collections.

How you hold data and use it is much to do with people, preferences and culture. The most obvious ways of dealing with data now is to use spreadsheets and databases. While these are both excellent systems, they can have the ability to deflect people from understanding what the information tells them.

At the above DC the initial refuse manager left, and was replaced by his deputy. The first manager loved showing data as graphical displays, and his data was shared with supervisors, drivers and all crew members. It was visually stunning, if not a bit too complex for some people to take in what it meant.

When he left his successor wasn't able to maintain those graphs, and so recording started to slip. The solution was to replace many of the graphs with very simple tables retaining the same data, but showing it numerically. He was happy, and the other staff all carried on learning from that data.

For every round there were the missed collection records for the whole year, right down to individual days. As a result of the ISO9001 registration there was full traceability for every incident on every round, including awareness of the crew composition every day. Every person was entered onto a skills matrix showing every round per day that they had worked on, and which they had a good working

Refuse and Recycling Missed Collections

Month	Properties	Collections	Misses	Misses/100K	Dfts.	% Default to Remedy	Domestic Weight kg/Qtr	Average No. of Props/Qtr	Weight Annual kg/Prop /Week	% Change Annual Qtr on Qtr
1999/2000										
April	64,000	42829	97	22.941	0	0.00%	10653928	64,061	12.793097	
May	64,061	43226	83	19.611	0	0.00%				
June	64,121	43623	64	15.108	0	0.00%				
July	64,182	44020	78	18.395	0	0.00%				
August	64,242	44417	63	14.844	0	0.00%	10733770	64,242	12.852522	
September	64,303	44814	64	15.065	0	0.00%				
October	64,363	45211	41	9.642	0	0.00%				
November	64,424	45608	41	9.633	2	4.88%	10271068	64,424	12.263807	
December	64,484	46005	31	7.277	0	0.00%				
January	64,545	46402	43	10.084	0	0.00%				
February	64,603	46782	46	10.778	0	0.00%	10700336	64,603	12.741003	
March	64,660	47156	39	9.130	0	0.00%				
Ave. for year	64,332									
Totals		5100092	690	13.529	2	0.29%	42359102	64,603 Annual	12.662343	
May to Sept.		2120099	352	16.603	0	0.00%				
Others		2979993	338	11.342	2	0.59%				
2000/01										
April	64,718	427536	27	6.315	0	0.00%				
May	64,775	427910	18	4.206	0	0.00%				
June	64,833	428290	18	4.203	0	0.00%	11396462	64775	13.533715	5.7892%
July	64,890	428664	21	4.899	0	0.00%				
August	64,974	429215	32	7.455	0	0.00%				
September	65,083	429929	20	4.652	0	0.00%	11057430	64982	13.089273	1.8421%
October	65,098	430028	15	3.488	0	0.00%				
November	65,245	430992	14	3.248	0	0.00%				
December	65,292	431300	20	4.637	0	0.00%	11277181	65212	13.302458	8.4692%
January	65,320	431483	15	3.476	0	0.00%				
February	65,404	432034	10	2.315	0	0.00%				
March	65,479	432526	16	3.699	0	0.00%	12502465	65401	13.654733	6.6593%
Ave. for year	65,093									
Totals		5159906	226	4.380	0	0.00%	46233538	65401 Annual	13.401387	
May to Sept.		2144008	109	5.084	0	0.00%				
Others		3015898	117	3.879	0	0.00%				

Annual % Change 5.8365%

2001/02

Client BRC already included 490
Amended to include Litter Bins 617

Month	Properties	Collections	Misses	Misses/100k	Domestic Weight kg/Qtr	Average No. of Props/Qtr	Weight kg/Prop /Week	% Change Annual Qtr on Qtr	Misses/ 100k/Qtr	Weeks
April	65511	418398	13	3.107						4.2
May	65542	438526	16	3.649						4.4
June	65598	438896	41	9.342	12017437	65550	14.1024183	4.2021%	5.4020	4.4
July	65608	438962	15	3.417						4.4
August	65643	439193	21	4.782						4.4
September	65672	419412	15	3.576	11522832	65641	13.5033246	3.1633%	3.9304	4.2
October	65712	459632	19	4.134						4.6
November	65735	439800	18	4.093						4.4
December	65753	399926	12	3.001	11778062	65733	13.7830336	3.6127%	3.7711	4.0
January	65791	480185	18	3.749						4.8
February	65817	400310	31	7.744						4.0
March	65891	420792	23	5.466	11092438	65833	12.9610444	-5.080%	5.5330	4.2
Ave for year	65689									52
Totals		5194030	242	4.659	4410769	Annual	13.5868885			
May to Sept.		2174988	108	4.966						
Others		3019042	134	4.438						

Note: PI requires May to Sept as one period and Apr plus Oct to Mar as other period.

2002/03

Month	Properties	Collections	Misses	Misses/100k	Domestic Weight kg/Qtr	Average No. of Props/Qtr	Weight kg/Prop /Week	% Change Annual Qtr on Qtr	Misses/ 100k/Qtr	Weeks
April	65954	421189	15	3.561						4.2
May	66011	441621	11	2.491						4.4
June	66049	441872	12	2.716	11320321	66005	13.1929146	-6.449%	2.9126	4.4
July		5949		0.000						4.4
August		5949		0.000						4.4
September		5678		0.000				0.000		4.2
October		6219		0.000						4.6
November		5949		0.000						4.4
December		5408		0.000				0.000		4.0
January		6490		0.000						4.8
February		5408		0.000						4.0
March		5678		0.000				0.0000		4.2
Ave for year	66005									52
Totals		1304682	38	2.913	11320321	Annual	3.29822865			
May to Sept.		883494	23	2.603						
Others		421189	15	3.561						

Annual % Change 1.3842%

Note: PI requires May to Sept as one period and Apr plus Oct to Mar as other period.

Note weeks per month to be altered

knowledge of. In that way we were able to utilise people safely, and generate supervision and training plans.

Each round was fully detailed for collections, in round order with any special collection details highlighted. Wherever a property had been missed, a flagging system was used to highlight the historic problem. If a customer had previously falsely claimed a missed bin, the driver would phone in to record no bin available as soon as they got that property, enabling a check by supervisors straight away

Drivers also took their role as team leader very seriously, if they had a loader who was not doing a fair amount of work, they would report that formally to get it investigated, and hopefully dealt with. The driver would record all anomalies during the day, and phone in any significant ones as soon as possible. This degree of detail and sophistication of processes is why they were able to become one of the most reliable services in the world.

This chapter so far has introduced PDCA, run charts, and the interpretation of data, plus an introduction to common cause variation compared to special cause variation. It also has reflected on the arbitrary, often ill informed nature of trying to rationalise every minor change in performance, and how that can lead to well intentioned disciplinary actions which will damage a service rather than improve it.

Other statistical methods available can now be brought in:

Flow charting of work is quite well used now, and there are several ways to do this. Rarely does flow charting need to be highly detailed, although every so often that is a benefit, for instance in realising the amount of redundant operations within a process, or if a computer system is to be altered, identifies how the ripple affect to other users needs to be flagged.

One of the simplest approaches to flow charting is to talk with the person(s) involved, and write operations onto a post it note. These can then be stuck onto a large sheet of paper, and checked against other people who are also involved in the process. The detail level can be quite high, or low, as needs be.

If more detail is needed, then a single part of the process, such as 'Process Pay' can be broken down via post-its initially, with option for 'if that happens', 'do this', involved and then drafting up the stages. Most flow charts can be quite succinct with only rectangles for actions and diamonds for decisions.

Other forms of flow charts can show where activities take place, perhaps department by department, or room by room. To see why it takes an average of 28 days to pay an invoice, simply tracking a piece of paper through an organisation is interesting. See where it goes, whether it does a loop in and out of some offices, which 'In trays' it stays in, and how much 'Value Added' some parts have. For instance if the Head of Service must sign every invoice, and there are 250 a week, what is the worth of that signature, does any single invoice actually get checked by her?

This sort of tracking can lead to a new vision for an organisation. Systems which are set up to 'control', are often the causes of failure.

Histograms are a very graphic way of seeing data. In the case study later, you will see the use of histograms to visualise failures, and then help to do something about them. Within 15 months of starting an improvement programme the failure rate was reduced to a third of before. This was largely done without computers, so that the ownership of outcomes could be taken on board by a low tech organisation.

One way of looking at it is Pareto analysis, named after the Italian economist who first identified that 80% of a problem is often caused by 20% of the issues. The 80/20 rule is often used, but not thoroughly understood for its potential impact on management.

I also use fishbone analysis, otherwise known as *cause and ffect* diagrams, or *Ishikawa* analysis. These are used to group areas of interest into manageable lumps, often directly related to one part of an activity, or a particular machine.

All these methods are useful, but the integration of how to use them is equally important. Some like to use quality improvement teams, to start new ways of working, or simply manage a new project. I have seen some excellent examples of how QIT sessions can help, and others where one person will dominate, and quash all inventiveness.

How many people have gone to a session where you are looking at a project, or setting up the business plan for next year, and someone suggests "Let's brainstorm the ideas?".

Again I've seen excellent brainstorming sessions where reams of ideas are written up on the board, and then no one has the faintest idea what to do next. The combined use of cause and effect charts and flow charts, enables some of the benefits to be unravelled.

Mind-mapping techniques can compliment brainstorming to show order and linkages of concepts, or be used as a catalyst for a single person brainstorm. Mind-maps can also help plan a lengthy document, such as a presentation of a research program.

The cause and effect chart below was used as part of an improvement process within a DC which was aware that much was in need of addressing, but was unsure of how to start the process. Having started with quality improvement teams, there was some disquiet as to what we could do directly, and what may need either board or client approval.

Undeterred, we brainstormed all the aspects of service delivery that could impact on the effectiveness, and then ordered (separated and sub-divided) most aspects of that session to create the cause and effect chart below.

This was plotted on an A3 sheet, and was used to fuel the next meeting, along-side the Pareto analysis for actual errors made. The A3 sheet actually had even more elements which had been reduced so that it may succinctly fit on a smaller page.

We decided the key areas affecting how good we could get were: Vehicles, People, Contract, Equipment, Customers, Site conditions and Refuse.

On the original sheet the area with the most entries was employees with 25 elements split into six areas as follows: Training, Information, Empowerment, Performance, Teamwork and Knowledge.

The Information area had: Round Changes, One off jobs, Performance, Special focus and Changes.

We were seeking to identify the characteristics of how to do something right, and then establish how to enable that. For the information

element we designed round information summaries as a guide to drivers not usually on that round, then inserted any special details each day in the correct position for the event.

The power of the fish-bone diagram is that a huge array of elements can be visualised at the same time, they can be sub-grouped into potential action areas and shared quickly with other people without getting over-whelmed by a massive report. Equally an arm of diagram such as 'Employees' could be used to create a fish-bone of its own, with even greater details applied when specialist HR staff could become involved – see the diagram opposite.

A more in depth approach to that case study will follow later. The benefit of a sheet such as that above is that you don't lose information inside a wordy report; you can pick on a theme and deal with it, and have the opportunity to see other parts of the scheme at the same time, seeking linkages and synergies.

Lastly for this area, flow charts can be used for a variety of reasons, I think that they are an excellent way to help manage the induction of new staff, please see the charts below for a refuse driver, which would be used with a linked set of short procedures. Consider the advantages of this, compared with weighty tomes on the do's and don'ts of refuse collection – see the following page.

These were improved on in time but this gives an idea what can come forward from a brainstorming session followed by the subsequent discussions based on the use of a cause and effect chart.

This was done with the supervisors, drivers and some loaders for refuse collection. Could you apply this in your offices?

More charts and ideas continue in the following chapters, and at the back of this book are a series of ideas for further reading, where you can follow up on ideas in depth.

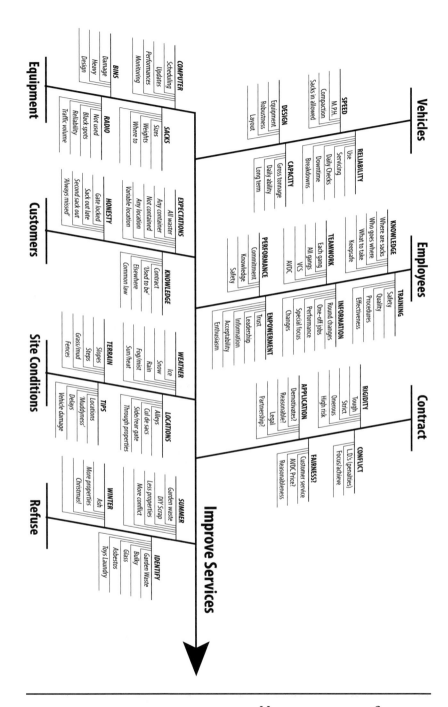

Vehicles

SPEED
- M.P.H.
- Compaction
- Sacks in allowed

DESIGN
- Equipment
- Robustness
- Layout

RELIABILITY
- Use
- Servicing
- Daily Checks
- Downtime
- Breakdowns

CAPACITY
- Gross tonnage
- Daily ability
- Long term

Employees

KNOWLEDGE
- Where are sacks
- Who goes where
- What to take
- Keepsafe

TEAMWORK
- Each gang
- All gangs
- VCS
- AVDC

PERFORMANCE
- Commitment
- Knowledge
- Safety

TRAINING
- Safety
- Quality
- Procedures
- Effectiveness

INFORMATION
- Round changes
- One-off jobs
- Performance
- Special focus
- Changes

ENPOWERMENT
- Trust
- Leadership
- Information
- Acceptability
- Enthusiasm

Contract

RIGIDITY
- Tough
- Strict
- Onerous
- High risk

APPLICATION
- Demotivates?
- Reasonable?
- Legal
- Partnership?

CONFLICT
- L.D.'s (penalties)
- Focus/achieve

FAIRNESS?
- Customer service
- AVDC Price?
- Reasonableness

Equipment

COMPUTER
- Scheduling
- Updates
- Performances
- Monitoring

BINS
- Damage
- Heavy
- Design

SACKS
- Sizes
- Weights
- Where to

RADIO
- Not used
- Black spots
- Reliability
- Traffic volume

Customers

EXPECTATIONS
- All waster
- Any container
- Not contained
- Any location
- Variable location

HONESTY
- Gate locked
- Sack out late
- Second sack out
- 'Always missed'

KNOWLEDGE
- Contract
- 'Used to be'
- Elsewhere
- Common law

Site Conditions

WEATHER
- Ice
- Snow
- Rain
- Fog/mist
- Sun/heat

TERRAIN
- Slopes
- Steps
- Grass/mud
- Fences

LOCATIONS
- Alleys
- Cul de sacs
- Side/rear gate
- Through properties

TIPS
- Locations
- 'Muddyness'
- Delays
- Vehicle damage

Refuse

SUMMER
- Garden waste
- DIY Scrap
- Less properties
- More conflict

WINTER
- Ash
- More properties
- Christmas!

IDENTIFY
- Garden Waste
- Bulky
- Glass
- Asbestos
- Toys Laundry

Improve Services

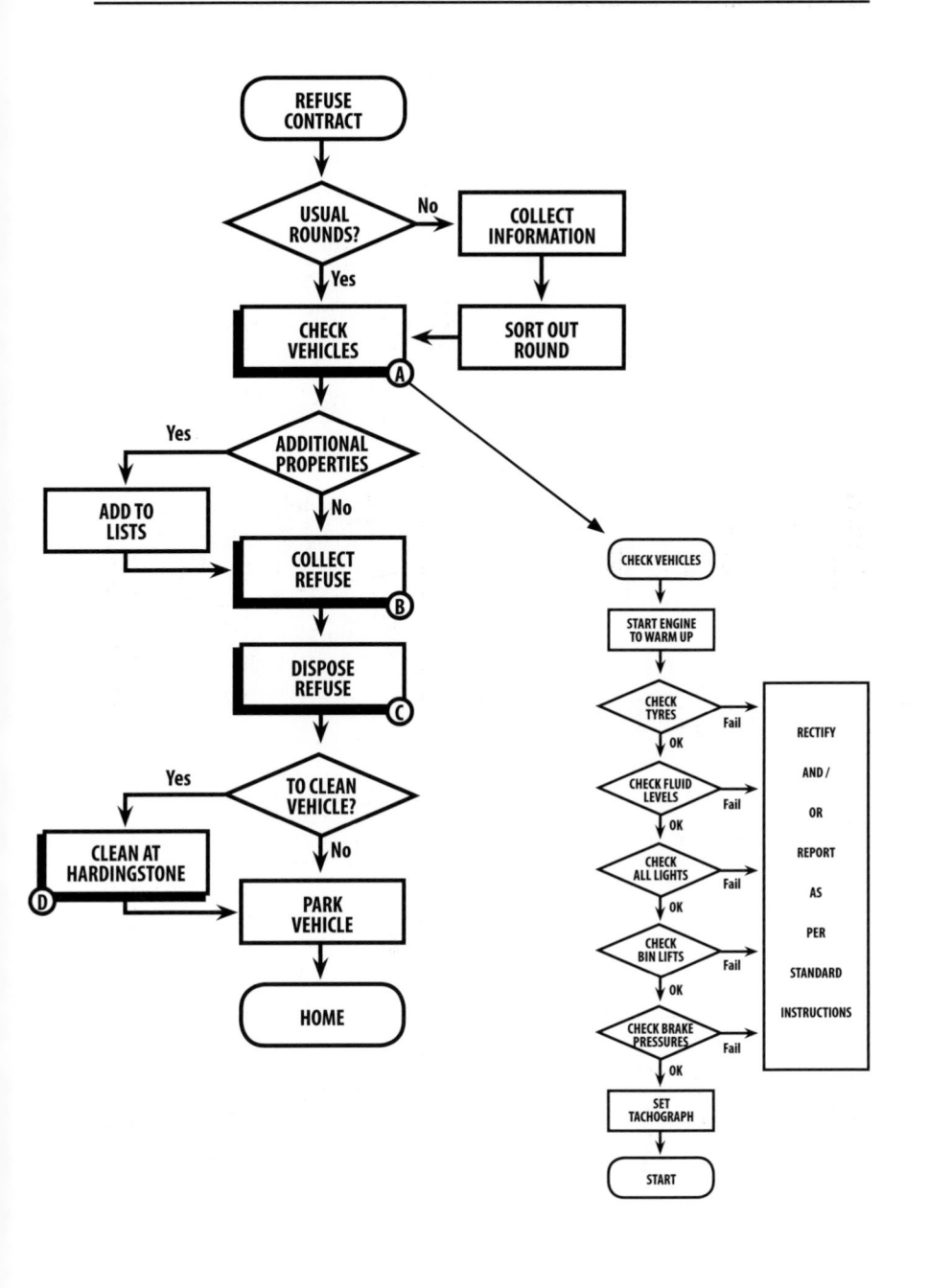

CHAPTER THREE:

Deming – His approach to people

W. Edwards Deming insisted on treating all employees as responsible adults, able to make a worthwhile contribution to their business. My experiences strongly back this up, in direct contrast to the traditional 'authority approach' of *Management by Distrust* (MBD).

MBD is an ailment within all councils and housing associations I have worked for. Standing Orders, Financial Regulations, Articles of Governance are all written on the basis that some people will misuse their position to achieve personal gain. So systems are built to cross check each other, which result in a head of service (HoS) having to sign 250 invoices a week. She can't initial them, use a rubber stamp, or do a random, value added, in depth check of a few. So the art of signing them off is to start at the top, and get them all done in 15 minutes before her next meeting.

She trusts the people who have prepared the batch that they are all genuine and correctly coded. But there is no value added by the process, just another few days added to the time taken to get them paid.

From a motivational point of view, MBD sucks! Tom Peters has made two telling observations on management for me. The first is that if a boss hangs around a subject long enough, his employees will realise the subject is a real one to concentrate on (Deming's Constancy of Purpose). The second was, "The vast majority of employees are hard working, dedicated, creative... until they get to work"

This chapter covers Deming's 'Profound Knowledge', a series of concepts whose beauty is their simplicity. Deming believed it would take a large organisation five years solid work to achieve CI (Kaizen) as he envisaged it. I have never headed the 'whole organisation' only Departments with up to 200 employees. Thus they have always had

to work within the structures and systems of the parent group. In every case that causes some degree of Sub-optimisation.

John Seddon (chapter 10) talks about the culture of command and control, where employees are not seeking to delight customers as their prime focus, but to meet the (often arbitrary) targets of their boss, in order to get a good performance appraisal, bonus, promotion etc. "Don't do the absolute best for your customers; conform to the expectations of your boss". There is some excellent reading to follow up on as at the end of this book, which gives a mixture of wider and deeper examination of systems than this introduction attempts.

Profound Knowledge

Profound knowledge is about building trust, belief, involvement, empowerment, awareness, commitment and a lot more into the organisation at all levels. The qualities that you expect from the shop floor, are the same qualities expected from the board room.

Everyone has a duty to add value to the business, and has the power to say, "This isn't right, we could do this better", and not only be heard, but also, if correct, to have that acted on. So the process adds to corporate confidence, people know they can make a difference, where-ever they are in the process. This isn't a corporate suggestion scheme, with a £50.00 reward for good ideas, nor is it an annual appraisal scheme, where once a year you have the chance at a 360 degree evaluation of you boss.

Let's start with Deming's 14 points, and then examine what they say and mean, with some of the synergies that come from them in combination.

Deming's 14 points are summarised as follows:

1. Create consistency for the improvement of product and service
2. Adopt the new philosophy
3. Cease dependence on mass inspection
4. End the practice of awarding business on price tag alone
5. Improve constantly and forever the system of production
6. Institute training and retraining
7. Institute leadership

8. Drive out fear

9. Break down areas between staff areas

10. Eliminate slogans, exhortations, and targets for the workforce

11. Eliminate numerical quotas

12. Remove barriers to pride of workmanship

13. Institute a vigorous programme of education and training

14. Take action to accomplish the transformation

These fourteen points were first put forward in Deming's book "Out of the Crisis" published in 1986. Full wording is at the end of the chapter.

Point four – with all the work following the debacle created by CCT, more and more contracts are now being awarded based on a significant weighting for quality. Private Finance Initiative (PFI) deals lead into very long term partnerships, and partnering principles are based on a great deal of initial effort to select the right partners, and then develop the right atmosphere for a long term win – win relationship.

Point six – a heavy reliance on training and retraining, makes sure that not only the immediate needs are dealt with, but also that longer term ambitions are prepared for. Combine this with *drive out fear* and *institute leadership* and the result should be music to the ears of every personnel officer.

Having worked for some excellent bosses, and then some bosses who are still bullies, it's easy to see which ones get the most done. If you fear your boss, you will tend to get done what they ask for, and usually when they ask for it. If you respect and trust your boss, you will do your best to give the best product possible, with some ideas of what else can be done, and often get that to them ahead of time. Respect and trust creates an inspirational atmosphere, full of positive energy.

Leadership is an interesting focus area, its not about managing or direction, leadership is about creating interdependent teams that will get on and do a great job without having to tell them how to do every little piece of work. They will learn from experience, make decisions, and focus on delighting customers. The leadership elements are about enabling, coaching, supporting. One of the easiest things to

learn from Deming is that it is the manager's job to eliminate barriers to people doing work.

These barriers can be many-fold. One that I worked hardest on was the emerging personnel handbook. 'Handbook' was entirely the wrong term as it was A4, running to more than 250 pages and still growing. Personnel systems are at the forefront of this litigatious era but, is it more important to bring in the *just in case* best practice, or to treat all people fairly with respect and give them a chance to really enjoy work? Many HR advocates fail to realise that their plethora of systems actually add to the costs of processes and increase the scale of management, potentially reducing long term value for money.

Best Value brought in the term continuous improvement, which has been added to by Gershon, and so it would appear that they (the government) must be advocates of Deming, for at point one, he has *Create consistency for the improvement of product or service.* The fundamental aspect of profound knowledge is to always improve on what you do. But then look at points ten & eleven, eliminate numerical targets, well that puts paid to BVPI's and also slogans, exhortations and targets for the workforce.

Much of Best Value depends on targets and the need to move your performance up into a higher band. Because of this, many attempt to fiddle the system. For example, you get ambulances to accident and emergency but don't admit patients because of timescales there. Is BV a reason why cleanliness is so much of a problem in hospitals I wonder? The BVPI's don't deal with 'clean' so its not on the performance manager's itinerary, nor a barrier for the chief executive to achieve the best score, and a performance bonus. Bonuses related to arbitrary targets are undoubtedly damaging to a business, or perhaps to the life and death decisions within a service.

BV breaks up operations into many discreet elements that do not necessarily create a useful holistic, integrated service delivery. When you look at point three, a new way of thinking is really needed. Without a dependence on mass inspection, how will all those performance m,anagers stay in place? Will the Audit Commission ever be needed again? Mass inspection is a legacy of poor performance: "We know you are not reliable, so we will check and correct everything you do!"

People who are inspected rely upon that inspection to ensure failures are corrected, and thus have no intrinsic motivation to do a reliable job. Inspection by others will generally create a long term worse service compared with self inspected services.

You must be confident that things are done right, and have ownership of what you do, but must every document, invoice, order, requisition etc. be seen by three people before it legally can go out? BV forces duplications, and worse, of processes if done ritualistically. How can you have high quality, reliable systems, without having management by distrust? Does it need a leap of faith? Or is there a systematic approach to managing risk?

Within a BV review for a housing association the pay and conditions of the workforce was altered to enable less paperwork, higher productivity, less inspection with an emphasis on quality and training, thus creating better value for money. The management and supervision had, for the most part, the highest regard to the quality of work done by their operatives. But when it came to designing the new levels of pre and post inspection, some were holding out for post inspecting nearly 50% of all work done.

The previous system of pay had been nearly 100% based on volume of work, whereas the new scheme was about 20% based on work volumes. And yet the management wanted to increase inspection in case of fraudulent claims!

I know that this pay method doesn't meet the aspirations of Deming, but it was a step forward from where they were. As it was a quick BV review, the focus wasn't on the ethical transformation, but how to meet the needs of customers better, increase revenue, and get better BVPI achievements.

Points nine and twelve work together nicely, in that they are both about breaking down barriers, one against the barriers to pride in workmanship; what does mass inspection do, if not to say to your workers, we know you do a good job, but we don't trust you!

As part of a learning organisation I think it's important that people go ahead and do their work, and where they are not confident that something is correct that they can go to a colleague or their supervisor to take advice, or to see if what they have done is correct. This helps

the person and team to grow, rather than relying on a system that forever lets them do it wrong, and be corrected up stream.

If people are worried that they wil be disciplined for making mistakes, they are likely to hide those mistakes. If you have a trusting organisation, they will tell you what happened, enabling them and the organisation to learn from them and develop better ways of working.

Many interventions by consultants can improve the way work is done in one work area, to the detriment of another work area. It's very important that people understand the context of their work within the whole area. Such as why some details are put on something in a particular way, what happens if something is missed off, or the writing is indistinct?

This is particularly easy to do within a computer system; a current process may be very fragmented requiring three different screens to be worked on before a simple invoice can be created, so the IT specialist integrates the functionality into one screen. The person can then do twice the amount of work in the same time, so everyone's happy, yes? Well often, no! Changing the way data goes into a database will often alter the ability to process or report that information elsewhere.

While Office A, is aware of the change, people in Office B, downstream of the change are not aware, so they will report a fault, if they are aware, and then an IT consultant will be paid to come in to see why the system has now become unstable. Such destabilising can be the life-blood of IT support departments!

If any changes to any working processes are ever to be considered, look at what you do, and how that affects people both up-steam and down-stream of the activity. This increases the corporate worth of the intervention, and often will help to identify redundant work currently done, not needed by anyone. Minor changes to processes can save over 50% of the time to do that work!

Lastly it is very important to have the consistency and tenacity to see this through, there can be early gains, and tangible advantages quite quickly, but it's the long term that makes the true changes, developing an organisation that learns, trusts, has joy in work, and gets better every month and year than ever before.

Look at this from a sales type of approach. Gaining a customer in the first place is one of the hardest parts of a salesman's responsibilities. Once you have a customer that trusts you, then repeat orders are quite easy, so salesmen know that their best long term plan is to keep those repeat orders coming in by delighting customers.

Local government doesn't have many areas where customers have a decision whether to buy from you, or somewhere else, but those powers are developing. The issue for LG is that a dissatisfied customer will create work for your departments, at the call centre and the back office. They will tell their neighbours, friends and work colleagues how ineffective you are, and from one incident, 50 people can get negative opinions of you. LG must concentrate on delighting customers, more than any high street shop ever needs to do.

There were four core values required by people to understand Deming's theory of profound knowledge:

1. Appreciation for a system
2. Some knowledge of the theory of variation
3. A theory of knowledge
4. Some knowledge of psychology

In addition there are cornerstones underpinning a business:

1. To stay in business and to create jobs
2. To expand the market
3. To continually improve
4. To grow intelligently

The meaning of 'profound' to Deming included: To have a deep insight, being intellectually penetrating, thorough and pervasive, existing far beneath the surface and originating in the depths of one's being.

From the above it is quite clear that 'doing Deming' is not like any toolbox techniques learned from reading abstracts of a book, it takes time, commitment and determination.

Very few managers understand their operation as a system, they will know the hierarchy of who reports to whom, and many of the aspects of what is done and some of the processes behind those actions.

While a systematic approach to thinking is not unusual, thinking of a service as a system is.

Take a break from reading, and try to visualise what your system would look like!

Well, that's a very traditional start to the normal way of working, each unit headed by an officer or manager, all reporting to a more senior officer. Every person has a good idea of what they should do, they have a job description, and there are rules and regulations to follow.

There is an annual service plan, cascaded down to sections and via annual appraisals; each person has their personal targets. The person contributes to the section, the section to the division, the division to the department, all cascading up into the corporate plan.

The cornerstone of personnel systems today are still based on mass production systems introduced by Henry Ford. There is virtually no redesign of management methods allowing for the pressures of our e-enabled world. Thirty years ago, people would write a few memos a day and have plenty of time for work. Now they deal with 40+ emails and spend much of the day in meetings.

Some organisations turned this on its head, with the chief executive at the base, moving up through the directors, to HoS, managers, officers and the front line at the top. A corporate statement of 'We are supporting you to get the job done!'

But where are your customers, where are the systems to work, how does the work get done?

Perhaps a more modern approach should be tried?

Both of these have a place in the way we work and think visualising linkages is a sound idea, enabling people to go to the right place at the right time. customers also is a nice warm and friendly concept, in most places seen as positive, except call centres, enforcement offices and complaints sections.

But work visualisation has moved on from here, these models are old hat, aren't they? All relationships have moved to partnering, with win–win concepts underpinning all you do!

So the next model may meet your thinking style!

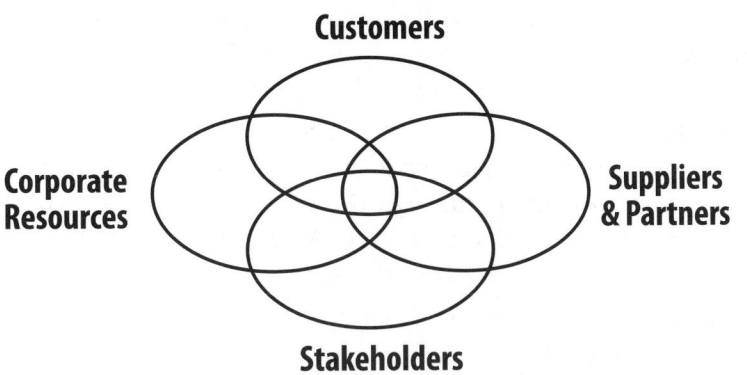

This infers more integration of services, with corporate resources overlapping with all the other interested bodies, so that synergies are created, risks are taken jointly and blame is not applied.

Deming took this another stage, but not with a simple symmetrical diagram. This is an alien way of looking at a system of work, and quite clearly this a system inside a factory producing goods, not an office providing a service, or an organisation carrying out street-scene services.

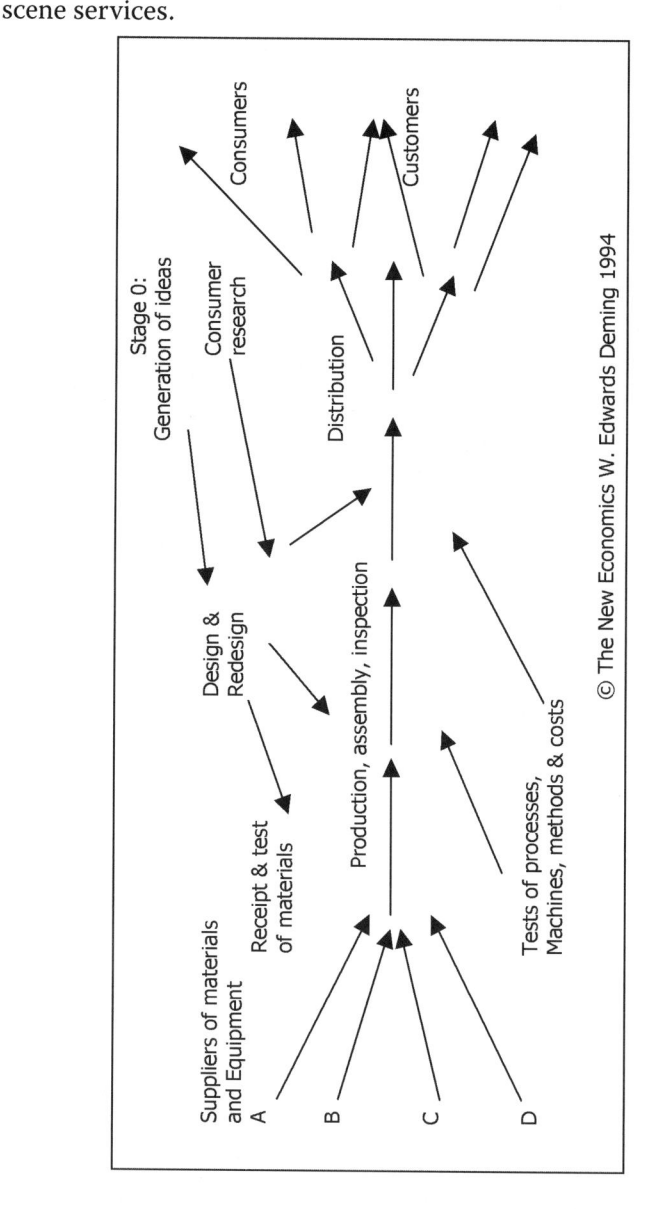

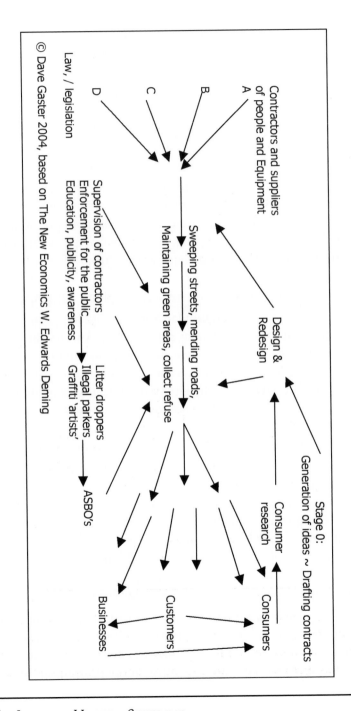

Stage 0:
Generation of ideas ~ Drafting contracts

Consumer research

Consumers

Design & Redesign

Sweeping streets, mending roads,
Maintaining green areas, collect refuse

Contractors and suppliers
of people and Equipment

A

B

C

D

Supervision of contractors
Enforcement for the public
Education, publicity, awareness

Litter droppers
Illegal parkers
Graffiti 'artists'

ASBO's

Law, / legislation

Businesses

Customers

Consumers

© Dave Gaster 2004, based on The New Economics W. Edwards Deming

Virtually all the work done by local government is either mandatory, and or, of an enforcement nature. So much of the above can not apply to LG, we are different. Well we are different, but all the concepts are transferable, you just need a translation in the middle.

It was the design of the above systematic approach that helped make a breakthrough as part of a BV Review (Cleaner Safer Places) for an inner London borough. I had been benchmarking the council against a host of other places. One of the most successful neighbours had massively stepped forward from it's near neighbours in terms of cleanliness, enforcement and reducing the fear of crime, but had achieved all that by spending twice the amount per head of population, or kilometre of street swept.

The tests in the borough I was working for proved that if we doubled our spend, then streets got cleaner. However, the amount of time they stayed clean was not impressive. We had a trial where a street had three people cleaning it all day long, six days a week, for more than eight hours a day. It got cleaner, but never stayed that way. Within 15 minutes of being almost spotless, it was getting dirty, after 40 minutes you would suspect it hadn't been cleaned that day, and within a few hours it was quite deplorable.

We watched the people in the streets, as with any form of normal distribution pattern, 80% of the rubbish came from 20% of the people. (Perhaps even less until the schools emptied, then the ratios changed). We checked the relationship between the provision of litter bins and their use. Where they were closer together, they were used more, although often by shop-keepers who should have been paying to have their waste collected.

We conducted attitude surveys in the schools, and found that 10 year olds were environmentally minded, likely to carry litter to put it in a bin, by the age of 15, it was more street wise to ensure you dropped litter, by the time people were around 21 they were more likely to put litter in a bin, if it were nearby.

When we watched behaviour in the street, we were quite surprised to see five year old children out with their parents, and all three drop litter, even when they were less than 5m from a bin.

At our neighbouring borough their streets stayed clean a little longer, partly because people had got used to them being cleaner, and partly because the enforcement and education was a little stronger, and more mature.

So our borough faced an interesting dilemma, increase the street cleaning budget by about £3M a year, or treat the whole street scene as a system. One where the traditional 'customers' of the service now became the prime focus; Seeking re-education, training, publicity, enforcement, co-operation as the main tools for moving onwards.

Partners at all levels were required, Schools, Shops, Market Traders, Police, Transport providers, big Businesses, Night Clubs, Pubs. Then integration of service delivery was a key. Being an inner London borough much of the public land was in its ownership or influence. The current cleansing regimes were split into hard contracts with defined boundaries. Wide footpaths would be divided along the centre running for hundreds of metres. One side of the divide would be cleaned by one contractor, the other side would be heavily littered but not scheduled to be cleaned for another day or so, and of course on a windy day, all gets shared out again.

The new contracts to emerge had to be based on the public realm, anything that could get littered, dirty or disfigured came into the joined up remit. Enforcement and supervision were merged, made local and interlinked with the local policing and localised cleansing.

The scope of environmental education became integrated and blurred with enforcement, the prime purpose wasn't to punish, it was to stop the need to pay for ever increasing costs of collection. So the prime focus went from making the contractors more efficient, and reorganising the Clients to better manage the contractors, to all working together, mainly at very local levels, to stop litter hitting the streets.

This was the start of a new paradigm involving a budget of some £35M a year once the Housing Caretakers, Parks Cleaning and Neighbourhood Renewal funds were taken into consideration. Seeing all the contracts, services and parties involved as entities obstructed a clearer vision that a system concept as in the box above enabled. Once that was clear, then solutions started to become obvious.

It should be noted that as an interim manager or project manager for an authority, I would not be recruited to instigate a new way of thinking and working throughout that body. I would be there to achieve their business aims as they see them, or help them to achieve a step change in performance (see later chapter). Throughout these interventions I would use many Statistical and People orientated aspects from Deming, but would not evangelistically be pontificating his way.

Where Clients have questioned me on methods, or asked me how I saw something in their data that they never had expected to see, I would show some techniques, and why the data talks so succinctly to me. The application of data analysis saved one council over £600,000 and helped achieve step changes in performances for recycling and missed bins. They were intrigued but not willing learners.

There are a host of other areas that can be discussed at length, but one must be "Joy at work", not just the fun of banter when the Boss is out, or the extra fun and games people can have to over-come the monotony and boredom of the daily grind, but actually coming to work, and enjoying the day.

"Joy at work" is probably the easiest way to get high performance, low sickness rates, inventiveness, and engagement. This aligns to driving out fear as well; people who are not under pressure to meet arbitrary performances may be better motivated and able to exceed those types of positions.

This must differentiate between arbitrary performance needs and business related achievements that are needed, to simply assume that everything would happen without plans, schedules and a Continuously Improvement philosophy a business could easily back slide in terms of productivity, customer care and competitiveness.

Thus 'Joy at work' is in no way an abrogation of responsibilities, it is simply stating that people who are happy at work, gaining real pleasure from what they do, are more likely to be productive. People who feel unduly stressed at work tend towards lower productivity.. Deming's 14 points and a summary of his thoughts on people involvement follow on the next two pages.

DEMINGS 14 POINTS:

1. Create constancy of purpose towards improvement of product and service, with the aim to become competitive, stay in business, and to provide jobs.

2. Adopt the new philosophy. We are in a new economic age. Western management must awaken to the challenge, must learn their responsibilities, and take on leadership for change.

3. Cease dependence on inspection to achieve quality. Eliminate the need for inspection on a mass basis by creating quality into the product in the first place.

4. End the practice of awarding business on the basis of price tag. Instead minimize total cost. Move towards a single supplier for any one item, on a long term relationship of loyalty and trust.

5. Improve constantly and forever the system of production and service, to improve quality and productivity, and thus constantly decrease costs.

6. Institute training on the job.

7. Institute leadership (see point 12.) The aim of leadership should be to help people and machines and gadgets to do a better job. Leadership of management is in need of overhaul, as well as leadership of production workers.

8. Drive out fear so that everyone may work effectively for the company.

9. Break down barriers between departments. People in research, design, sales, and production must work as a team, to foresee problems of production and in use that may be encountered with the product or service.

10. Eliminate slogans, exhortations, and targets for the work force that ask for zero defects and new levels of productivity.

11a. Eliminate work standards (quotas) on the factory floor. Substitute leadership.

11b. Eliminate management by objective. Eliminate management by numbers, numerical goals. Substitute leadership.

12a. Remove barriers that rob the hourly worker of his right to pride of workmanship. The responsibility of supervisors must be changed from sheer numbers to quality.

12b. Remove barriers that rob people in management and in engineering of their right to pride in workmanship. This means inter alia, abolishment of the annual or merit rating and of management by objective, management by the numbers.

13. Institute a vigorous program of education and self-improvement.

14. Put everybody in the company to work to accomplish the transformation. The transformation is everybody's job.

People in Continuous Improvement

		CUSTOMERS Stakeholders External / Internal	VISION	EMPLOYEES Leaders/ Coaches	Demings chain reaction

S T Y L E

Leadership		Listen, Coaching, Supporting, Enable, Strengthen, Remove Obstacles.
Teamwork		Work "cells", Cross Functional, Quality Improvement, (incl. Suppliers/ Clients)
Flexibility		Multi Skilled (adaptable), Trained (Safe), Cross cover- (Scope, skills,documentation)
Customer Focus		Know your Customers, (How to Delight them; Make their needs your Objectives)
Constancy of Purpose		Concise Vision (Fully Communicated) Known plan to achieve;Generate Loyalty and Enjoyment; Don't panic.

Improve Quality

Costs decrease because of less rework, fewer :- Mistakes, and snags: better use of machines and materials.

I N F O R M A T I O N

C O M M U N I C A T I O N

Verbal	LISTEN: Ad- hoc, Opportune, Team Briefings, Meetings (Balanced / Open) Enable: Up, Down & Across!!!
Written	CONSIDER THE READERS!!! Letters, Memos, Reports, Bulletins.... (Openness, Succinct, Charts, awareness)
Computer	Easy use / Access: Reports (Meaningful, appropriate, timely, adaptable). Data (Summaries, trends, graphs)
VISION	Target Your Future (OPEN, FRANK, ACHIEVABLE),Direction and Goalposts.

Productivity Improves

Capture the Market with better Quality and Lower price.

F U T U R E

People	TRAINING: By "buddy", Internal, external, seminars and college. Personal & team and inter- team SKILLS, METHODS, KNOWLEDGE, DATA, REHEARSE, PERFECT.
Skills	Broaden abilities, new areas, x-cover, leadership, technical, legislation, I.T.
Products	How & what to improve; Product / process, new products, better tolerances, new materials, innovation.
Customer/ Supplier Links	Go to suppliers & customers, see how they work & use your products. Have them join your teams, create

Stay in Business

Provide jobs and more jobs.

©Dave Gaster 1995 **Greater Accuracy Shorter Times Exact Requirements**

CHAPTER FOUR:

Continuous Improvement as it should be

While CI is at the heart of Best Value, and is even tacked on to ISO 9001, neither of these is what I call CI nor the position which the Japanese call Kaizen. While front line staff would need to be aware of BV and even, to a certain amount ISO 9001, they would not be active in the daily improvement of services as part of their routine.

Kaizen is the attainment of all the people within an organisation working towards the improvement of the way it works. Clearly BV does not achieve this while some performance managers gerrymander with work to make it look better than it is. The cleaning staff in Hospitals know where they could do better, and if they were fully involved with, and committed to, the absolute best care of patients they would make suggestions, do things in different ways, and add a great deal of benefit.

In the worst cases of CCT these cleaners would be given a schedule of what to do and when, regularly told by the contractor to do what the spec says, and claim if more was wanted. Don't get involved with the nursing staff nor the patients. Do what you are paid for and nothing more!

If cleaning staff were missing, then most of the cross cover could come from someone who already had a day's work to do. If they were cross covering someone who had special responsibilities, such as a super clean in the operating theatres, would the cross cover people be trained to that standard, and would they have time to do it?

How far beyond that sort of scenario has BV taken us? This being the end of the second term for this government! Studies on the spread of MRSA have shown that mops are one of the easiest ways of moving it from place to place. A learning organisation would understand this, and take measures to ensure that the cleaning process actually eliminates infections in each area, and isn't one of the prime causes.

Within the remit of CI you should have committed staff that care about what they do, and want to make a positive difference not only in the short term, but also in the long term. The benefits of in-house service delivery are many, as can be the dis-benefits. Having learned about Deming in the early 90's, and achieved training and commitment for a very strong core of management and front line forces which created a critical mass, we decided to do CCT differently!

We had to win our contracts in competition, and to do this we involved either the whole workforce, or representatives throughout the process, creating inclusion and commitment. We would win the initial contract basically on price to begin with, but later as CCT improved we also won it on quality. For one contract the client advised that it would set the best tender submission for quality at 100%, and then assess the rest against it. Any tender submitted not making a 60% score would be eliminated, without looking at the price.

We did our homework, and answered every question posed within the invite to tender. An external assessor who had been evaluating tenders for years declared it to be the best quality submission he had ever seen. None of the other tenders would have achieved 60% compared to it so the client officers fudged their results making them get a little over 60%, rather than face difficult questions from councillors as to why those contractors got on the short list. They then awarded the contract to us after an expensive process of compare that wasn't needed by their own rules.

Here is where we were different, if we said we were going to achieve a target we did it! In fact we did far more than we predicted, we massively improved reliability measured in missed bins, rectification of faults, jobs on time, monitoring report details to the client. Overcoming problems, providing out of hours cover, organising resolutions that should sit with the client, doing things quicker than were required, always and reliably.

In reality, over the length of a contract we would improve dozens of service delivery issues, so that customers would expect that as the norm. By improving the quality of what we did, we made fewer mistakes, and so had less cost for rectification (Within a tender bid

we allowed a cost for getting things wrong, if that wasn't needed, we could invest it in improving the specification)

Thus when the contract was due to be retendered we would strongly suggest that the new contract should be specified to how we were actually doing the work, not the lower specification that sat behind that. Thus much of the better specification would go into the new contract, together with higher requirements for performance.

We still had driven down costs during this process, and thus our competitive position had improved three fold, we were doing a better specification of work, to a higher level of certainty, for less money. Thus winning the contract next time was far more likely.

We also worked to the minimum profit margin possible, which in time we reduced to ¼% advising the council that the difference between our tender and the next lowest was their 'profit share'. We were then extremely well positioned to pick up work from housing associations and to build up external work via Trade Refuse and Garage Services.

This all sat perfectly within the 'Deming Chain Reaction'

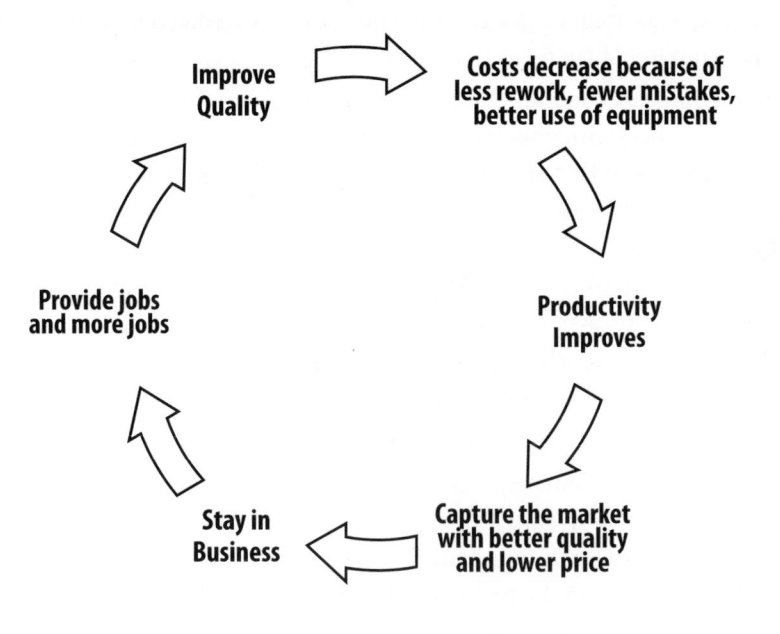

Every DSO that I have headed has:

- Grown rapidly via tender success
- Improved service delivery
- Reduced costs (on average by 14%)
- Dealt with exceptional circumstances very well
  (Major floods, hurricane, coastal oil pollution...)

The initial work (pre Deming) was partly because the opportunity to improve was so great, the latter work was much more focussed, and achieved the upper quartile performances and business transformations needed by today's society.

Looking at the chain reaction above; starts to make a lot of sense once you get your mind round it. If an organisation has a fund to pay for what goes wrong, then it must be able to invest that fund in stopping that going wrong. Let's say you have an annual budget of £50,000 for rectifying poor work. Every year that is spent on rectifying work, and you never address the causes of those problems. If you make a determined effort to improve work, perhaps by working harder, or longer, things may improve, but you will still make those mistakes and then correct them.

What if, instead you look hard finding some opportunities to improve, and make those improvements, then suddenly some of that £50,000 isn't needed. But be careful, just stopping doing things wrong doesn't save money on its own. The old story of Taylor's Law is very right in many places; the amount of work to fill a whole day is proportionate to the amount of day available. If you simply make it easier to do work, then people can get lazier as a result.

You may say that you have no fund for correction of work, and while that may be true in abstract, are you saying that no mistakes are ever made, and that they take no time at all to rectify?

Within Housing Maintenance I had a good performing organisation, which just needed some positive leadership, and a real sense of direction. It had been twin hatted until I arrived, that is there was no distinction between the team deciding what to do, and the team doing the work, so many of the client/contractor aspects were evolving.

I was learning about Deming after my building maintenance officer had showed me an article entitled "BS5750 or Deming?" I was hooked on the theory, but needed to bridge the ideas into a DLO within a traditional LG set up.

Let me show you some of the things we did describing the affects that we created from a business and service delivery perspective. Many aspects being done then would now be described as a partnering style of approach, I don't think we applied a label to it at the time.

Getting Started

Applying "Deming" within local government was not straight forward. Standing Orders and Financial Regulations made the setting up of partnering arrangements quite difficult, thus careful thought had to be applied where awarding of contracts was not primarily based on price.

What was more important was to address change management styles, looking at information smarter, involving people in their own destiny. Once it is felt quite certain that there was a capability to move forward, the leadership team "advertised" their desires to get better, and asked their employees and customers what they should be doing better, how they could make it easier to do their various jobs?

As you could guess that lead to a number of suggestions that were not exactly what they looking for! But there were a great many ideas that were very worthy of pursuit.

Housing Maintenance is much more complex to run than it would first appear. From the "Direct Labour Organisation (DLO)" side of the equation there are several thousand properties to maintain, within a fixed annual budget, meeting an array of legal, and timed requirements, in a customer facing, sound business ethic.

These DLOs are very akin to production lines in some ways, in that they have between 10 and 100 thousand works orders (discreet jobs to do) a year, and each one has its own time constraint, varying from a few hours to 35 days. The problems are multi-fold as each works order is independent of every other one, and they can be worth £5 to £3000 each.

The majority of works orders were initiated by people who have not seen the job, or where they had, they hadn't lifted carpets, nor floor boards to see the extent of the damage. If you then include the occasional storm, or flood which create many more works orders, you can start to see quite how "fluid" the style of management needs to be.

Thus the plan of work established each morning, was never the same as that which was actually done by the evening. Yet on average a hundred jobs will be complete, many of them, not known of first thing. Thus there are tremendous opportunities to get on the path of CI, if the partnerships can be sealed in every direction.

One of the features of "applying Deming thinking" to a business, is to understand variation, and by understanding it, bring in methods to reduce the impacts. So what adverse affects of variation are there in Housing Maintenance? From a customer point of view, they would want the right job, done well first time, on time, preferably with only one person coming to the home once, not several people all doing their one speciality.

From a client representative point of view, they need to be well informed, with jobs to time, all changes of demand met, and stay within budget. From an employee point of view, they need a safe environment, with the knowledge, tools and materials to do the work, communications to enable rapid change and empowerment to do the work actually needed, rather than work to the details initially provided.

Approaches and actions

Within this DLO there was considerable emphasis on "Quality Circles", with a guide taken from the National Society for Quality through Teamwork (NSQT). Initially all interested parties were given 1-6 days training from the British Deming Association. That enabled an array of ideas to be generated for what would be "Essential, nice, helpful" to address, these were taken from all stakeholder positions, other than "independent customers", with whom the DLO were denied contact by the client. To cover this we used employees and their relatives who were also tenants. Teams were former to develop ideas, with a facilitator assigned to each team. These teams were

deliberately seeded with widely focussed people, to provide views from several perspectives at all times. There were members from "the client", stores, vehicle maintenance, managers, unions, supervisors, administrators, and all crafts – electricians, plumbers, carpenters, bricklayers, painters, and even the dreaded ub-contractors sitting and working next to employees)

Communications became vital to support all the processes. It was quickly learned that nothing should be done without a position report of what each team was doing and where it may be going. The old Chinese whispers had to be overcome. The various teams found themselves documenting much more, which for projects would include; who was in charge, who was involved, where the major jobs were.

For major work they discovered it was better for all concerned to draft a "quality plan" addressing order of work, organisation and responsibilities, personnel, procedures, special processes, works instructions, inspections tests and plans, audits, records and amendments to the quality plan. This was years before a review of the construction industry brought in an almost identical plan for major works. But these were wanted by the workforce so that "They knew where they were". This gave a greater strength to the position, as the workforce would have seen this as an imposition if it had been mandated without their own request.

Some of the most important work with the client officers included process mapping the whole of the works order flow, from the initial call from the customer, to completion and payment. It was an "eye-opener" for the client, as they knew their process was complex, but then found that the DLO side was about three times more complex. That shared knowledge help move forward a direct link of computer systems, to both receive and complete works, to enable a good variation system, (so that discretion could be used on site for altering work), and to develop tighter quality delivery measures.

One such measure was to develop a "Skills Matrix". A plumber should be able to do all routine plumbing tasks, but some couldn't do specialised work, or for instance fit a side panel to a bath, earth bond the pipes, put on a skirting board, and paint it. Thus some works

needed four people to visit, on occasions some twice, such as to fit a bath.

With the skills matrix, the DLO paid people based on their ability to do the whole job, thus reducing the time taken, the inconvenience caused, and at the same time saving costs. The matrix showed the range of complete ability, with three other categories: "wanting to be trained, part trained, and trained, supervision required." This was a real "Win, win, win" position for all involved. They also used this data to help standardise van stocks on vehicles. Most tradesmen had an individual van. Their core trade lead to a stock (with all max/ min levels of stock) with additional items for each of the additional skills listed in the skills matrix.

Lists started appearing all over the place, showing investigations started, solutions being considered, changes proposed, and dates for implementation. Some lists required "Stores" to address issues from operatives, and others showing what Stores wanted from operatives. Both of these could easily impact upon administration. In some ways this lead to a fast-track for an information organisation, where they could spot the cause and affect of most occurrences in the various areas where it may be possible, and through that started eradicating potential causes for delays and new work came on stream.

Within 18 months they had changed or improved:

- 35 systems in "Building Works"
- 10 systems in Vehicle Maintenance
- 22 systems in Administration.
- 9 systems in Stores and Purchasing

Starting on Partnering

During this period we also had a considerable increase in workload, as the client decided to accelerate their improvement plans via the DLO, and we also won three major Planned Maintenance Contracts during this time.

We needed to be able to do more work, and do that work more efficiently. We were stuck inside the normal financial regulations regarding three quotes, formal contracts etc. So I spent time with

the Heads of Legal and Finance to get Standing Order's and Financial Regulations altered so that any work tendered for by the DLO as a prime contract, had all supporting supplies and sub-contracts deemed as being tendered.

Thus we no longer had to develop a huge paper chase for every supplier, enabling longer term win–win arrangements to develop. With supplies to stores this enabled more time to be focussed into buying smarter, rather than a huge administration process.

A particular emphasis was given to the payment of invoices, which with tracking and flow charting was brought under greater control. This cut the reliable payment period to under a week, and allowed improved supplier terms to be negotiated.

We repeated this with our sub-contractors. One came to the fore in particular, forever able to do good quality work reliably. As time went on more work was completed in shorter times, with fewer errors.

The increase in work volume was quite phenomenal, and as a result, we started to make significant profits, as the fixed costs were over-recovered from the work.

Benefits to customers?

The organisation was quite good before they started all this. They did most work right, had won all the major contracts, and were gradually expanding the business through contract success. customer satisfaction with their work was running at 88%.

But we were aware that 12% of customers were not satisfied, too many of their jobs became overdue, we were a little inflexible in how we did work, and had paid liquidated damages for going over time on some contracts.

Within 18 months, we reduced costs by over 10%, (partly through rapid growth in turnover), had less than 3 jobs per 1000 that needed remedial work, costing under £70 per 1000 jobs to rectify. Liquidated damages reduced from some £10,000 per annum to zero. customer Satisfaction went up from 88% to 96.5%. One really nice aspect of the change was a client monitoring report, which showed we had completed 85% of emergency works before the client had raised a works order on the computer.

During this period we kept a log of all improvements made, to remind ourselves of the journey, and to keep a reality awareness to what we tried to achieve.

We were required to write an annual business plan as part of the wider council involvement. The Plan was completed on time (this being the first one for us), and had no arbitrary targets set. It had financial objectives and budgets, it sought improvement, but no specifics such as we will increase customer satisfaction by 5%.

Improvements were shown generically, 'We will carry out at least 20 service improvements within Housing Maintenance,' was the closest we would get to arbitrary targets. The chief executive was delighted with it, I'm pleased to say.

The above process was carried out at the same time as we addressed refuse collection, vehicle maintenance, street sweeping, plus replacing our IT systems, and setting up a new depot.

One of the most astonishing pieces of work at that time was by my vehicle maintenance manager, he was involved in the Refuse development ideas, and wanted to try some ideas himself. So he started looking at the costs of tyres for the Refuse Fleet. Each Refuse Compaction Vehicle (RCV) had ten tyres, costing about £250 each at that time.

Refuse collection isn't kind to tyres as its all stop/ start, turning, scraping kerbs and then going onto a tip face twice a day, with a dubious off road arrangement to the tip face.

He started to try different ideas and after a while came to me asking what more he could do, and how we could learn more from this. His work was brilliant and the later developments equally good. We reduced our tyre costs by over 60% as a result, achieving almost unheard of miles per tyre, and a knowledge of our pence per mile costs.

The final scheme used the tyres, kept them at the right pressures, turned them round on the vehicle at the right intervals, had them re-grooved once they got to a certain depth, and re-moulded after a certain amount of wear.

Each option was tested and costed to see what the optimum was. This is not the sort of activity that I would expect to see arise from CCT nor BV. The manager in question later went on to a major tyre firm, as a senior manager, offering transport fleets a managed tyre provision at an agreed pence per mile basis. In his first year, he outsold the whole sales department for the unit he was based at.

Returning to refuse collection, I mentioned earlier that we used a Pareto analysis to evaluate where to apply our energies to really make a difference in delivering services to customers. The results achieved in under 18 months were staggering, taking us from one of the better organisation to among the very best in the world.

This shows a stunning turn round in performances, with a 66.5% reduction in errors made achieved in less than eighteen months. The statistics speak for themselves.

Refuse Remedials by Cause ■ 1991 □ (1993)

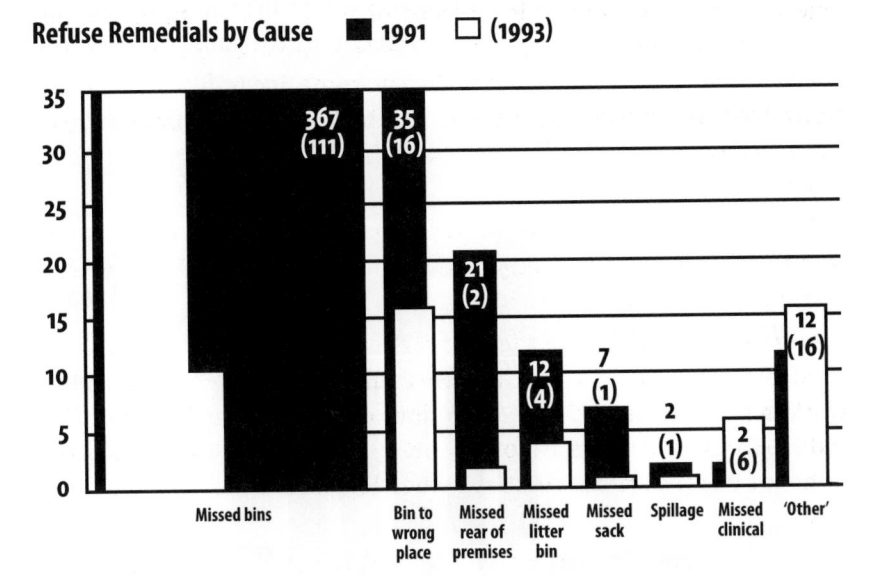

	1991	1993
Average Number of Properties	28,350	29,000
Bins Lifted	1,480,000	1,510,000
Remedials	459	157
Percentage jobs as remedial	0.031	0.010
Operatives employed	21	22
Tonnes refuse collected	26,200	27,400
Remedials per week	8.8	3.0
Missed collections per 100,000	24.8	7.4

We analysed the initial data in a variety of ways and the two real eye-openers are seasonality, and the benefits of Pareto thinking.

The graph below showed something we just hadn't registered before, that the vast majority of remedials occur in the summer months.

Monthly Refuse Remedials ■ **1991** □ **1993** ◇ **Refuse Tonnes**

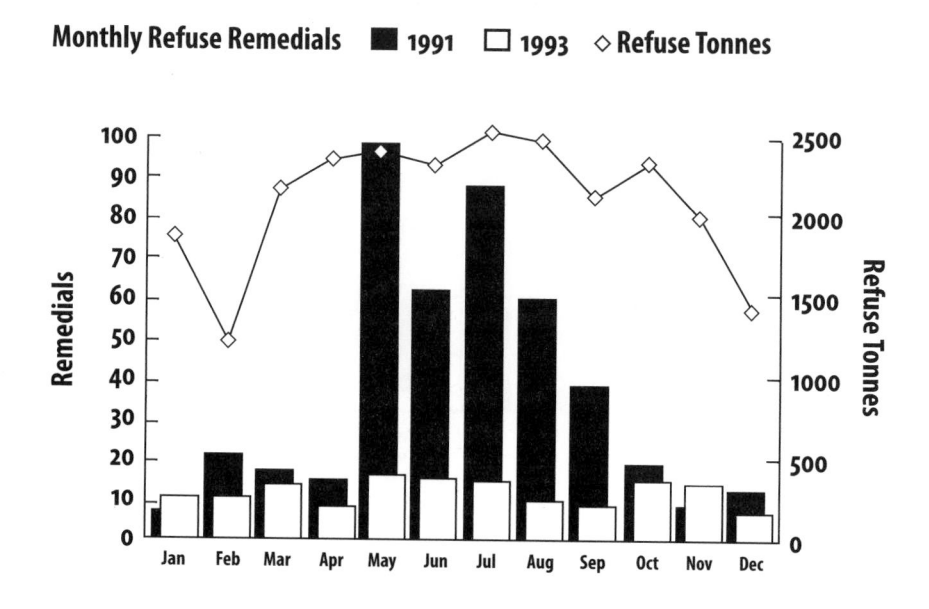

Combined with data from brainstorming and the Cause and Effect charts, it became clear that one of the greatest causes for failure, was holidays, with less experienced agency staff to cross cover.

This was made worse by the very high volume of garden waste in the bins leading to the occasional injury from straining arms, backs and thighs.

The last graph shows the variations between the rounds, in the earlier year four rounds had about one remedial a week, while two rounds

Refuse Remedials ■ 1991 ☐ 1993

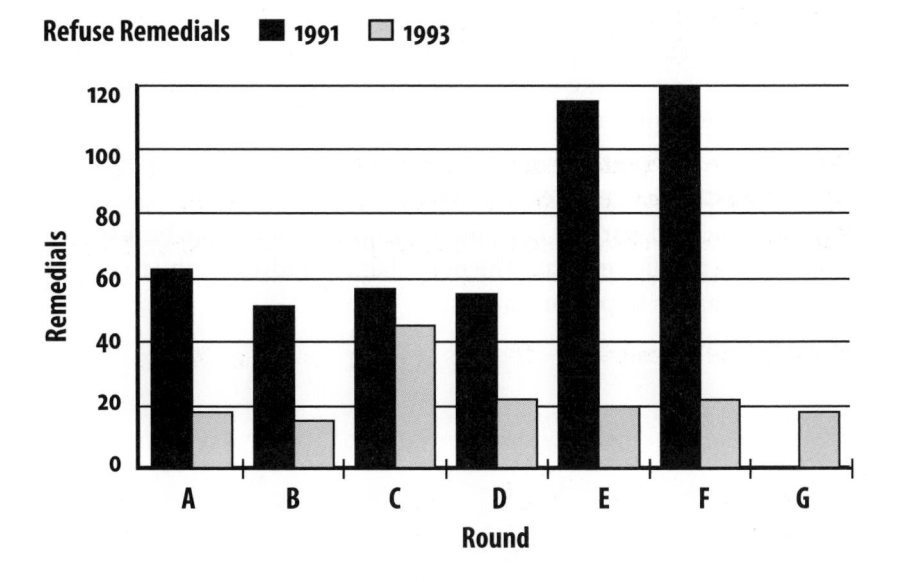

had in excess of two remedials a week, not quite an 80/20 rule, but something like one.

Having worked on the causes of problems, altered methods of working, and added a smaller round due to growth in property numbers, it is clear that all rounds are greatly improved, with most having less than one remedial a fortnight. That saved each crew the inconvenience of returning to another location, and saved the DSO the costs of administration, fuel and vehicle wear etc.

This work also led to us undertaking a review of safe working procedures for wheeled bins. We discovered a fair proportion with

over 100Kg of waste in, mainly as a result of people stone-picking their gardens and using the wheeled bin as a wheel barrow. When a bin was this heavy it could:

- Cause an arm to wrench out of the Shoulder
- Make the operative over-rotate the bin, causing a spillage, or an injury in trying to stop it
- Cause a lower back strain

We investigated these issues against a possible RSI scenario, (Repetitive Strain Injury), and introduced procedures to minimise that risk, resulting in less injuries, and lower costs. [Less agency cross cover], which with some other aspects made the additional operative and round self funding.

Both these examples are quite some while in the past, they were repeated with even greater long term benefits at another authority. But, as indicated earlier, continuous improvement can be used in part, or for specific reasons. The next chapter addresses the use of CI for Step Changes in performances.

CHAPTER FIVE:

Continuous Improvement to create better service delivery

So far I have concentrated on the blue collar services associated with CCT, and while CI is very successful in these areas the potential for transformations elsewhere is far greater.

Areas with significant potential for both service and value for money improvement include: Administration, Finance, Information Technology, call centres, Contract management and Enforcement.

Call centres, are often hailed by the government for making a real difference in the way councils deal with the public and I can only agree. They do make a real difference but often it's in the wrong direction and they end up reducing the quality of service and increasing costs.

I'll pick out some snippets from my assignments by way of example, and while all my assignments have been to improve service delivery, none of them were commissioned to look at the CC initially, most authorities thought that their CCs were adding to service delivery, if not reducing costs.

Call centres are one of governments 'Bright Ideas', but do they add value? Well in my experience, they generally do not. I have been directly involved with four call centres, one during creation, and three when they were either developing or 'semi-mature'

Call centres (CC) are a good idea because:

- They provide a professionally trained interface for communications with the public
- They can have powerful IT solutions to manage call progression CRM; (customer relationship management)
- They can have longer opening hours than individual services
- There can be flexible levels of staffing to match forecast demand peaks

- Waiting times for calls are managed, and failure rates are 'managed'

However call centres can be bad ideas because:

- They take customer contact away from service providers
- They reduce the flexibility, strength and influence of the back office
- They usually add to overall costs
- They usually monitor the wrong stuff
- They can add to the contractor costs, by instructing the wrong actions
- They can make services gradually get worse, and yet have a powerful CRM to show control

The first CC I was involved with was at a fairly well performing DC, with most services delivered to customers being of a good standard. This was linked to a government scheme, trying out a single Gateway to DC and other government services. It went in with a blaze of publicity, and with a number of painful decisions. The back office support to services, such as planning, were stripped down of admin support, both the backroom areas and CC had some teething problems.

There were high levels of customer contact, far higher than expected, a great many vociferous complainers, high levels of stress, and high levels of sickness. The result? The high level of contact "must be positive, people have easier access to the council and therefore it must be good". It was already dearer than forecast, but under-staffed, so more staff were recruited, and the Director of Resources lost her job.

At a London borough, a fairly youthful CC had been running for about nine months. It was seen as a success, and had been at the front end of an integrated reorganisation to create better services for customers. One of the prime motivators had been a BV review where the Auditors were critical of customer handling, but mainly the monitoring of calls and closedown of jobs (recording they were done, rather than just doing them)

The CC was bright and airy, had a very good CRM, and they were (as always) monitoring the call handling. The initial training plans were sound, and all their PI's were being met, BUT, the service to the customers was getting worse! The reason? Well the contract for Refuse was in its last year, and they (the contractor) just weren't trying any more, and the borough had upset them as well.

As an interim manager you learn to listen to the brief and compare that to personal findings. The contractor was committed to doing a good job, so why were services 50% worse now than a year ago?. Nothing matched up, the contractor was ISO 9001 registered, with a commitment to continuous improvement, they recorded the same data as on the CRM but showed better results! Their data looked sound, and so did the CRM, and yet they were different. So an exercise of 'compare' was needed.

The contract was clear, a missed bin reported prior to noon had to be put right that day, and one after noon, had to be rectified by noon tomorrow. So where were the differences? First we looked at the data, then the interfaces for communication.

The data mainly showed differences in:

- Time of receipt
- Numbers of properties affected

Both affected performances, the data was transferred by an automatic fax, straight from the CC to the contractor, with no involvement of the refuse 'client managers' at all. The contractor dealt with urgent stuff straight away, and recorded all transactions on a spreadsheet, and had had to increase admin levels to handle the imposing pile of paper (two A4 sheets for every fault).

The 'errors' in the system were numerous:

- The CRM only polled to the contractor hourly, so jobs raised after about 10.50 arrived after noon and thus was not needed to be rectified until the next day
- The CRM defaulted to the current time, so if calls were handled rapidly, and put on later, the contractor got them late, with a far earlier time frame intended.

- If a call related to whole Street, that may be put in the text file, but not the contractor fax (thus only one property would be collected from, then ten other complaints would come in)

In addition the CC focus was on handling calls quickly, but rarely addressing the honesty of customers. Two customers down one street had reported missed collections 17 times between them, that was three times more than the rest of the street, and it was a long street. An on site investigation showed that their property lay-outs were quite standard, so no reason to miss them. The Refuse management and contractors worked together to check for 'waste not out' prior to collection. Within five weeks both had been found to be falsely reporting they had been missed, when they hadn't bothered to put waste out for collection on time.

Meanwhile ther contractor feed back about 30 sacks a week of domestic waste from individual properties, languished in the CC. Once the communications between client and contractor had been restored, these were investigated and many became Trade Waste customers, decreasing the costs of Domestic Waste, and increasing income. A hit list of suspect properties (who had reported frequent problems) was generated for the CC, and the number of false reports started to diminish.

A few operational issues were also recognised and dealt with such as estates blocked by building works, and alterations to parking control causing vehicles to no longer park half on the footway, thus blocking narrow roads to heavy lorries.

Missed collection levels were improved by 40% in weeks, levels of rectifications within contract times dramatically increased, contractor costs reduced, and client income increased. The attempts to get the CC to monitor causes of failure, and volumes of 'Repeat Calls' was very much a lot of effort for little result, as their PI's were about speed and delays and call drop outs, not adding value.

At a medium sized housing association the call centre was small, bit disproportionately large for the number of calls taken. It was the brainchild of the chief executive, and very much a 'no go area' for the consultant. But like so many CC's it was the cause of many operational problems.

The CC had high levels of staff turnover and most had little technical knowledge of the services they were supporting. Specialist housing diagnosis tools were under-used due to a combination of lack of training and the desire to ensure that the PIs on call handling were met. The 'supported services' couldn't trust the CC to add value by raising accurate job tickets, and make appointments, so they avoided this by using the CC as a recording service mainly, and then calling tenants to diagnose repairs, or make appointments.

There was an added point of interest, in that there were three levels of urgency that could be used for works orders; today, one week and four weeks. Either work was raised as 'today', or the computer default for one week would prevail. All small work was issued direct to a specialist small fast-track team, and thus far too much work was done immediately, adding to costs, but keeping the customers satisfied.

The best solution was easy: close the CC, have a reception and switchboard, place two people in the response maintenance section (RM) as repairs clerks, use the 0800 number straight to these clerks, place other people in sections needing dedicated admin, save costs of duplications, increase the capabilities of most sections to do the work with greater flexibility.

The above was too radical, and likely to cause the chief executive to blow a fuse, so it was recommended to remove the barriers to working together, create a physical proximity, and then a centre of learning within the CC, which would migrate out to the others. Have the CC staff do some of the paperwork for RM, plus carry out post completion interviews for small work via telephone monitoring for work quality, get them to use diagnosis tools by getting assistance from RM officers, go out to a few jobs with operatives. In short get involved and understand the business.

This gave the capacity to handle 90% of all calls first time, making appointments to do emergency and small works, or to have a surveyor check out the situation. Service improves, calls reduce, costs reduce.

The last CC was in an inner London borough. It was large compared with the others, and handled calls well in a multi-lingual community. It dealt with loads of admin support services, and as far as we could see, added value. The client departments in charge of contracts

interacted with the CRM data to potentially use it to good affect. The client department was in serious need of positive management, but its weakness appeared to precede the CC set up, which is partly why the CC added value.

With all these examples the organisations undervalued the ability to share data electronically. The last one was some way forward, but still had too many interfaces which started with electronic data and converted it to paper, then back to electronic data again.

The true 'expert' for call centres is John Seddon at Vanguard, (www.lean-service.com) or if you want to become an expert yourself, try reading "Freedom from Command & Control – a better way to make the work work"

The real problem for most organisations is that a CC causes a lack of contact between customers and the service providers. For most issues that doesn't really matter, if you want to get something done, or rectified, and you call a number and that resolves the issue, then it is convenient and efficient.

Where this doesn't help customers or the business is where an issue is complex, unresolved, or repetitive. One case that I was discussing with a software company, was that their CC was taking many many calls for the same problems, which meant that there was a simple fault on the system that their programmers could rectify. After the first couple of calls were received a workaround was recommended by the software engineers, and staff at the CC went through explaining this to hundreds of callers.

The CC monitoring showed that they were dealing with the calls well, and that most customers were satisfied. But, from a 'computer system provider' reliability point of view, hundreds of customers were aware that the system had an unresolved fault.

The support engineers were unaware of the scale of the issue, as it hadn't been escalated to them other than as a one-off. When they became aware of the fault, they were able to design a fix, and migrate it to all their customers, quickly and at low cost.

As an experiment they trialled having an engineer in the call centre to see what issues were arising, so that they could start working on

improving systems directly instead of handling hundreds of calls daily about the same faults.

The results were startling, and as they found a series of minor quirks, they were able to diagnose causes and resolve the issues immediately. Calls to the CC started to reduce, as most of them had been repetitive, and customer satisfaction levels with the Company started to increase quite quickly.

From a personal point of view, I have had to do battle with several large companies as a direct result of their inability to properly deal with customer care. Think about your own problems from a customer's viewpoint and relate this to how your service may be portrayed.

I will cite only two: The first was a Carpet Sales business, which sub-contracted all the fitting to others. We ordered a fairly expensive carpet for hall landing and stairs. This was a big and technically demanding job.

The fitters arrived late, at 4.00 in the afternoon, looked shabby, and were a little threatening to my wife. The quality of fitting was abysmal, and it later transpired that the experienced fitter was off sick, so this was the fitters mate plus a friend. The work finished after 8.30 in the evening with a huge clean-up needed to see how bad their work was.

I called the manager of the carpet shop the next day, and they sent out someone who tutted a lot, agreeing that the work was sub-standard, with lots of "I don't understand this, they are our best team" type of statements. Then it became clear that this nationwide firm sold the carpets, but sub-contracted responsibility for fitting, allegedly not having a contractual responsibility for the fitting. The person who came out wasn't empowered to make a decision, and this had to be seen by the manager, so I asked why he was here, rather than the manager?

The manager had only been involved in carpets for a few weeks he had managed a supermarket before that. He came, looked, tutted, and agreed the work was poor, which is when we discovered that the 'proper' fitter was off sick on this day. They agreed to buy extra carpet, and insisted that the initial team had to do the fitting and stretching. I said that the dye colour would be different; they insisted

with modern processes that it would be identical. Weeks later the carpet arrived, and was a totally different colour.

So I tried their national call centre, which is when this went from bad to impossible. The CC could handle simple routine calls, and refer you to the local shop, or to procedures. The procedure says, "fitting is totally down to the fitters", so I had a dispute with them.

The CC was called "customer services" according to their web-site, and it had a CS manager. The CC staff were rarely allowed to go to their supervisors, and never allowed to escalate anything to the manager. When I asked why there was a customer services manager who wasn't allowed to talk to customers, what was his job then? I had silence!

Eventually I had the full cost of the carpet refunded, and paid only for the fitting. This took weeks, and made me convinced that if only the managers and CC could add value, then it would have been resolved in days, and at less cost to them than the eventual outcome.

The second dispute is with a huge provider of internet and multi channel TV. They have no linkage between sales, accounts and the CC other than awareness that a service is being provided. Both my sons have signed up 'special' student deals for a combination of services, and the installation of services has been nearly good.

The contract would be quite clear, services X & Y for £39.48 a month, paid by DD on the 9th of the month, job done! Well, no not quite!

Despite having terminated the contract and service over eight months ago, they show the service as being reconnected the next day, and cannot stop billing for it. Many months after repeating the mistake, a solicitors letter was created to chase the invoice created in error. The company wasted huge effort and costs doing the wrong things progressively worse!

For my second son, this was, and is, a nightmare. They agreed a price, written on the contract, and they are to take this via DD. Sales don't tell accounts the pricing of the deal, so accounts invoice the standard amounts, not taking it via DD. We challenge the invoice, and they tell us they don't know the correct price, ask lots of questions, and in the meanwhile terminate the services.

So far there have been twenty phone calls to them, four terminations, and two letters, neither acknowledged. A phone call can wait in their queuing system for over an hour, and at the end of such a wait, they then have lost me as a caller. There are two parts of the service, one is now on a DD at a higher price than it should be, the other is currently free! We expect the next termination soon.

What is the cost to a service provider that can not resolve simple issues after twenty attempts from a customer to link their businesses together? Both my sons are going to other providers next year!

I think you will see from the above, that I will never be a fan of call centres which monopolise the customer interface for a business; they ostensibly look like a good idea, and can get a BV tick in the box, but gradually do irreparable harm to the service.

Returning to service delivery in authorities, I previously have criticised two aspects of traditional management systems within an authority but not followed them through to any extent, one is management by Distrust (MBT), and the other is Command and Control. (C&C). The first causes duplications, and a lack of ownership of responsibility for any piece of work, as someone else will check it. The latter makes the boss more important than the customer.

Earlier I have shown how some partnering arrangements enabled better service delivery at lower costs. At a later district council I worked for, we replicated many of those arrangements, and would pay sub-contractors invoices on a Thursday, if they were correctly presented to us by noon on Monday. The sub-contractors were diligent about the accuracy of invoices, and worked for us at about 9% lower than they would work for the client!

To achieve this partnering we had to overhaul our processing capabilities, and retain that level of service when people were off on leave and or sick. This was achieved through an awareness of what a real challenge to procedures can achieve. The real processes here were learned through a training opportunity, which is easier to appear in this book, the real life processes were similar, and took a few weeks from start to end, the training session is more compact for inclusion.

In 1994 I attended a three day course called "The Prism Experience". It was high power, quite intense, and extremely good value for money. Towards the end of the second evening we started on a mock trading system, to deal with customer enquiries where demand exceeded capacity to deal with calls at first. We would run the simulation, analyse what happened, then redesign the procedure for dealing with the calls.

This was using all the methods as in chapter 3, with constant redesign using the PDCA cycle.

The first run using what seemed to be a very logical system, with people all working in their own departments and handling the enquiries as quickly as possible went into a complete meltdown, it became swamped by demand greatly outstripping resources.

We redesigned the methods to do the work, and on the second run took an average of 11 minutes 5 seconds to deal with a call, although the time to deal with each call increased throughout the exercise. So we went back, reviewed the data, found the causes for delay, re-designed the systems, and went into run three:

The system came more into control, other than one special cause event, the capacity to deal with calls remained constant, and the average time per call was reduced to two minutes 26 seconds. Everything was recorded, and we found that where we had made 7 errors in the initial run, there were none in the third run. So again we reviewed the data, analysed the causes of delay, and altered the system for doing the work.

On the final run we averaged 62 seconds a call, with no errors, no special causes. The longest any call took was less than 90 seconds, when the shortest call duration on the second run was 4 minutes.

If this were real life, and you could do work with a supplier that completely satisfied your needs in 62 seconds, instead of calling you back ten minutes later, would that feel better? From your own service delivery approach, if you could improve your ability to handle work more than ten fold, would you be interested. How important is the customer to you? How important is Value for Money for you? Are these two areas more important than C&C or MBD?

The chart also introduces the upper and lower control limits, which effectively shows whether a process is in statistical control. The second run was not, as the process went on through the day, the queuing time to do the work increased. As the process design improved, the reliability to do the job got better, and the capacity to do more work improved.

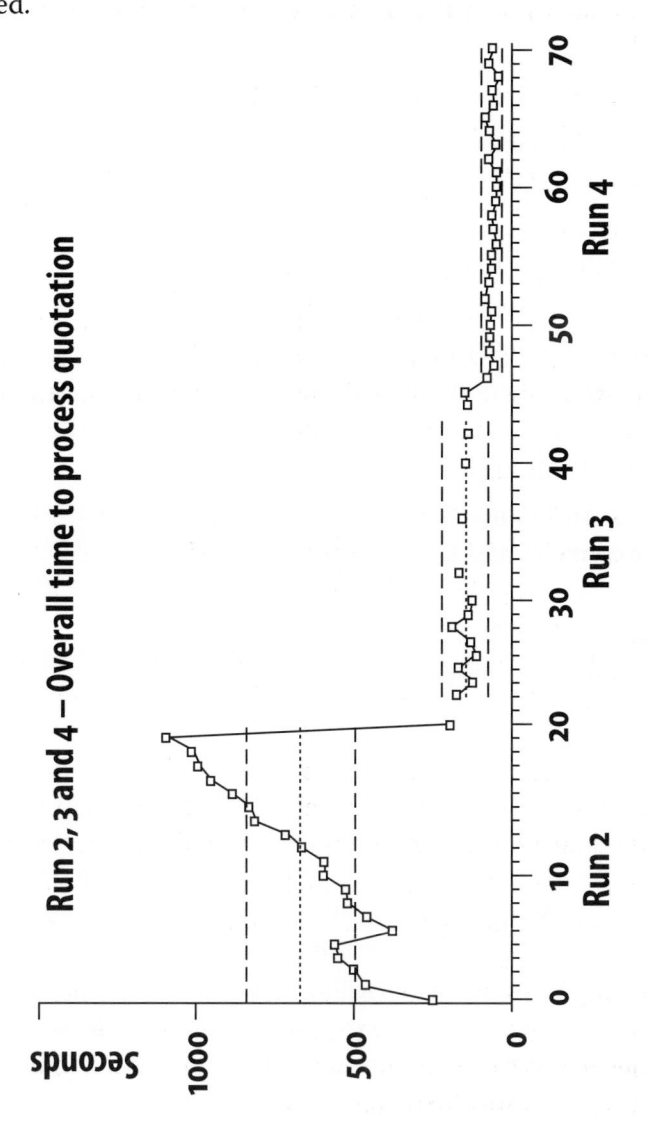

From a practicable position, the first two runs of this process were stressful as demand exceeded capacity, and as the day went on, people would be literally tearing their hair out. The latter two scenarios were much more like fun, in control, and felt like doing a good job.

These types of examples can be repeated for virtually any activity where there is a repetitive process to be carried out.

There are masses of examples regarding the appropriate use of information, to give some credence to this consider the list below:

* Housing Maintenance – Improved 4 DSOs
  costs reduced by 14% on average
* Housing Maintenance – Always improved
  service delivery to upper quartile (UQ)
* Housing Maintenance – Fast tracked appointments
  scheme, from inception to UQ in 4 months
* High court litigation – Resolved significant dispute via mediation
* Contract Dispute – Resolved in customers
  favour, £600K below budget.
* Refuse collection – Achieved UQ services in
  three councils, and step improved another
* Recycling – Step increased from 4% to 19% for
  same overall budget (overall 28% increase in
  service delivery within same net budget)
* Tyre costs – Reduced by 60%

At a housing association with good performances, it took three months to make them UQ, with 100% response work on time. Investigating their performance management systems showed a high degree of incorrect monitoring, reporting and recording work. Carrying out an audit on the causes of failures alone improved their apparent performance on overdue emergency work ten fold.

One of the strengths of recording information on spread sheets is how quickly you can re-organise data to learn new facts, or compare data from one source to another. The most innocuous of reports have yielded stunning information.

I discovered that a DSO was allowing all its drivers to take materials straight to tip every day. A driver and mate would drive ten miles to tip, off load and return at the end of day, having offloaded less than 60Kg of material. This was happening many times a week, but usually with only a few teams. They always had these reports, but never thought about what they could learn. By sorting it by weight of load, the five worst crews were identified, and the practice ceased, the saving would potentially add up to tens of thousands per annum.

At another authority the contractor, who had half the Housing Maintenance workload, decided to not extend their contract, leaving it at short notice, with no TUPE transfer of staff to our DLO. We were given the work, and a backlog of over a thousand overdue works orders. So we had the task of recruit, restructure, induct, and manage the backlog on top of the day job.

We set up additional reports to mange the backlog, and at the same time, cut the average days to do works, while reducing the amount of work being done late. It took us just over six months to go from a dire situation to UQ. At the end of that process we added in an appointments scheme which took four months to become UQ.

We were using a fairly basic financial and management system, which was robust. We added a data abstraction tool to take the information into Microsoft Access, where we designed our own reports. With all the management team trained to CI working, making that data 'sing' was relatively easy.

An easy aspect for managing data is to set up works orders not done by priority and age. The oldest batch of jobs are targeted each day / week, with the affect of quickly reducing the average days to do jobs. With an inherited set of really old work it was interesting to note the affects of these. Ten jobs that are 180 days old mixed with ninety jobs that are ten days old takes the average days up to 30 days each; even though 90% are done in ten days!

One area where I was not very 'Deming minded' was where my building maintenance manager would create reports, but then not use them to their fullest affect. Whenever he saw me walking to his desk in the morning with a bundle of paper, he would know that there was more to learn. But we were a very good team.

That manager has since moved into the private sector, running building maintenance according to a framework of control systems which have amazed his employers, and earned him two sizeable promotions as a result.

The earlier examples for refuse collection DSOs are interesting. The first one, where I completed my work in 1994 is still amongst the best in the country, but has slipped a little from 7 misses per 100,000. The latter, is retaining a world class service at around 2.9 misses per 100,000. This proves that where you take CI seriously it is sustainable!

CHAPTER SIX:
Step Changes in performance via Continuous Improvement

Continuous Improvement is designed to create long term, sustainable improvement into an organisation. There are a number of ways this can happen, the three most frequent are likely to be:

1. Internal sponsor/manager starts the process and sees it through
2. External consultant is engaged to change the way of working
3. Interim manager/project manager is taken
   on to do a discreet piece of work

These can occur in isolation or combination. The latter area is where I am most frequently involved, I am not normally engaged to introduce Continuous Improvement, nor to 'do Deming', I will be in for a BV review, or post BV review, prepare for an inspection, or to make a planned project a reality.

In all of those cases, I will not start from any form of template, but there is a process to follow; listen to the brief and question it for full understanding. Put things into perspective, understand performances and ethos, then start looking for what is good, and what can be built upon, enabling a plan of action to be drafted.

All the techniques of CI can apply, PDCA, involve and listen to people, investigate systems, seeking their potential and areas of weakness, and analysing information in a scientific way. No rocket science, and rarely anything different to many people can do anyway. It's a bit like cooking, if you have some ingredients, and a really good knowledge of food, you can create a masterpiece. In this case the ingredients are data. Information gleaned from a number of areas and put together carefully to understand what it all means.

Step Change can do an incredible amount, quite quickly. For a Call Centre getting overwhelmed with calls, it could reduce the pressure ten fold within days. For an accounts payment team, it could transform

services from 10% of payments taking more than 28 days, to all done in 14 days, and then get better.

The projects I have been involved with are usually bigger, and more tangible. For instance to transform service delivery in the collection of refuse and recycling sound mundane, but consider the following:

This contract was in the North of England for a small district council which had just received a poor BV Review showing poor prospects for improvement. They had entered into a Partnering Agreement with other DC's and two contractors, the refuse collection was via their DSO and the Head of Service was on long term sick.

They were running out of time to start a change from an 'Anywhere on property sack collection service' to a planned wheeled bin collection with a box collection for recyclates.

The consultant was recruited to head up a project to enable top level performances within tight budgets. Within a month the scheme had been evaluated and a presentation to full council where it gained unanimous support from the hung council. The specification was altered from one 240 litre bin plus one 60 litre open box, to a standard 180 litre bin, and two 60 litre lidded boxes. The price obtained for the 180's being far more competitive than forecast, enabling the change.

The purchase of wheeled bins, vehicles (Refuse and Recycling) plus recycling boxes were fast-tracked to conform with Standing Orders and European Procurement directives, while negotiations for Round Restructuring went ahead. The recycling vehicles were already on order via the Partnership, but the final designs and layouts were considerably modified for operational and safety efficiency.

The rounds were re-structured using the council's GIS together with a Database designed and built by SSD (Support Services Direct Ltd.) in partnership with IT Pro- Solutions. The whole process from commission to the first rounds being operational took under 5 months. During that time new Pay & Conditions were agreed with the workforce, allocations to rounds sorted, and a recycling ramp designed and constructed within the main depot

Then there was an unexpected closure of a local tip, and direction to a tip further away was potentially very difficult to bear, as this added

to daily journey times, thus reducing the amount of time each crew could actually collect refuse. But the DC was able to persuade the County to alter its plans so as not to jeopardise the achievements at that point. Severe weather and massive recycling participations both added pressure to the start up of the scheme.

The council agreed that there could be considerable operational flexibility to have a fixed overall nett budget, with variable resources, including the sales proceeds of the recyclates together with their recycling credits from the County, and a considerable increase in Trade Refuse income (due to a step increase from wheeled bin customers, and the elimination of incorrect historic free trade services when charges should have been applied)

Overall the council moved from 4% recycling to 19% in a year, for no additional budget. The forecast is that the service can achieve 24+% recycling once all operational and enforcement issues are settled.

The service was later commended both as part of the Partnering initiative, and by IDeA with a page dedicated to it on their website.

There were several levels of data handling, enabling all the Refuse and Recycling rounds to be fully detailed and co-ordinated such that the level of service delivery was never compromised. Not only were the rounds restructured, but so were the accounts, enabling a clearer vision for monitoring change, plus cause and effect of proposed changes.

The degree of involvement with office staff to manage the process was high, and the refuse drivers and loaders were quite stunned to have a series of 7.30 meetings to help design, and gain ownership of the changes. There were tough decisions, and several levels of re-examining time tables and planned schemes, and it was delivered on budget, on time.

I have previously mentioned the legacy of doubled workloads and a backlog of 1000 out of date works orders within Housing Maintenance. This was a step change of a type, as were several aspects of the inner London BV review for Cleaner Safer Places.

However, the last area I will address under 'step change', is a London borough as an examination of their recycling achievements. This

borough had made some early solid progress in recycling, and as a result had a very stretching mandatory target. They had continued to invest in more and more recycling schemes, with some award winning ideas, but very little growth in recycling.

They were aware of a huge array of reasons why people didn't recycle, most of which were genuine. Each time another target was to be met, {The better each local authority recycled in the late 1990's the higher their mandatory target for 2003/04. Thus neighbouring councils may have targets of 9% and 25%, the latter a penalty for trying too hard?} they rolled out another scheme. They were also fairly adept at playing the BVPI game, and in one area achieved UQ status through a relatively low cost, if not tongue in cheek concept.

As part of their review I was seeking data, with a view to Benchmarking that against other systems. Getting good sound data proved quite difficult, with request after request being apparently ignored. So I did what I should have done earlier, ignored the chain of command and visited the officers doing the work.

They had such an array of data, analysed in so many ways, many of them looking very impressive, that it was puzzling why I had had such a problem getting very little. It turned out that the performance manager didn't ask for the right information, with too many management Silos in place compounded by the fact that the various parties were all quite content to row their own boats.

I started to evaluate this data against finances and the benchmarking information, and a very obvious, but startling fact came out. All of the recycling schemes that were in use were resulting in precious little recyclates. Most were less than 20% efficient and could with some work be made 70% efficient over time, for little more investment than current.

I spoke with the waste manager, head of finance and department head; they all had an inkling that this could be better, but no idea that for little more expenditure they could improve outcomes by 250%. Their current budget bid was for several hundred thousand pounds, to do yet another scheme. I suggested that for say £70,000 they could unleash the potential of their existing schemes.

Their motivation for their proposed scheme was that exceeding a certain weight of waste disposal to tip would cost them £200 per tonne excess (this 'fine' was latter reduced to £150 per tonne). I pointed out to them that they were paying far more than that per tonne for recycling, and that could reduce to under £60 if they changed their core interest to participation, effective services and greater operational efficiency.

The scientific application of statistical analysis can be applied to economics!

CHAPTER SEVEN:

Best Practice can be a hindrance

There are a number of institutions that hold up a scheme with almost that salesman pitch, of "Do this and you will be assured to dazzle your neighbours..."

Ideas can be cloned, adapted and adopted from place to place. BUT, you must understand what you are doing and why. What works perfectly in one authority with their systems, people and customer base, will not necessarily work at all well somewhere else.

Local government and housing associations are not franchises like McDonalds, where every eating experience should be the same, whether it's in London or New York or Bath. The differences between Authorities are sometimes subtle, other times very obvious.

Just because 'Sheffield' has an extremely good CC (I've no idea if they have), it doesn't automatically follow that the same solution will implant perfectly in Timbuktu.

When dealing with CC's earlier I showed that three were reducing customer services while increasing costs, while one appeared to be adding value. The last one was a very well run CC, with a person who had business flare managing the unit, against a series of very poorly managed silos being supported.

The other three caused a barrier to service, and increased costs. When considering installing or expanding a CC you should really explore how dire a position you are in, and look at the worst case position of the CC getting bigger, the back offices failing to cope in their slimmed down structures and contractors possibly being alienated from their Clients.

One in particular led to a greatly increased level of transactions, more costs, and a really variable affect on service delivery. The back office affects were strangling all departments, and with latter budget restraints the CC got bigger and significant slimming down of other

areas had to occur. Effectively this one decision heaped enormous pain on the authority over a period of years.

So take extreme care when visiting Beacon sites under the BV banner. Yes you may be able to largely clone that system, idea or approach into your organisation. But before you try it, test the water, remember the PDCA cycle, see what will work or what will not. If you want to be a little more traditional, run a brainstorm session, and try a SWOT analysis on the idea if you feel comfortable with that, or preferably with a fish bone (Cause and effect) analysis.

Some Beacons have achieved that status via very sound processes. I was talking with the heads of two quite different organisations which have achieved remarkable specification changes to be among the Best in Britain for recycling diversion.

The first had been chipping away with ideas, consultations and partnering, and are probably one of the best 5% in the Country. Part of the process taken had been straight out of the best practice of PDCA as espoused above, but the manager had never heard of Deming.

The second had simply spoken at length and visited with a neighbouring council, who was also among the best 5% in the Country, virtually cloned every aspect of the operation, and used a specialist manager to force through all the difficult aspects that arose. They are not far behind the best, and could get a little better. Where they did very well was to 'foresee' all the potential problems, discuss them at management team and cabinet, got firm political support and assembled a team of well prepared staff to hammer through the changes. They knew it was problamatic, so they prepared their ground well to deal with all issues.

It's the same with any form of transformational process. If it's a *one size fits all* solution, will your size fit it? Business Process Reengineering was all the rage 15 years ago, loads of places did it, only to find that around 85% of interventions failed.

Perhaps you favour the European Quality Excellence Model, as it gives a template for many areas of your service, and enables a self audit, so you can plot your progress over time. There's no doubt that this will help some people, but does it give you all the keys to unlock those barriers that cause inefficiency and failure?

One last favourite is to become a black belt at Six Sigma, this has been one of the areas creating the most outspoken, rantings about how best to destroy a good business. But freedom of choice must be yours.

Any pre-assembled template will have gaps, assumptions and the potential to create a 'them and us culture divide'. Those that are 'black-belts' may not empathise with those that are not, and too many constraining conditions will be forced through as needed.

CHAPTER EIGHT:

Performance Management

Try to avoid 'doing' performance management from the centre of the organisation outwards. This can create a culture where the centralists feel all powerful, the edge dwellers feel undervalued also rans.

performance management must sit with the teams that are doing the work. The information needs to be as near as to 'now' as possible, and they need the tools, capabilities and empowerment to do something about it. Ask yourself a few questions about the information you are managing with:

- Is your information up to date?
  - Should you have some data every day?
  - Does the performance vary from day to day, or at certain times in the day?

- Is your information accurate?
  - Did you ever do a reality check on it?
  - Does all the information correlate correctly?

- Is your information detailed enough or too detailed?
  - Can you make strategic decisions reliably with what you have to hand?
  - Can you pick up supporting information straight away?
  - How does what you see, measure up with benchmarked data?

- Can you see trends, or are they common cause variation?
  - Have you been given a monthly description that adds no value to data?
  - Have any of your charts got upper and lower control limits shown?
  - Do you use run charts, or only have data in tables?
  - Do you have so much data that it looses you?

- If you had to make an important decision today,
  can you do that without more data?

- Would you be able to verify that the data you are using is correct?

Adequacy of data is to some extent a personal thing. In four Authorities in a row I have had external auditors check BVPI's and go away quite quickly, having been able to tick all the boxes, and test the supporting information without qualm.

At one council the auditor was stunned at the array of reports, and the ability to analyse it from so many viewpoints, asking, "How can you manage with all that detail?", I pointed out that we were Upper Quartile in all areas, and reversed the question, "Why can't others get everything to UQ?".

The amount of data I want to see is huge compared to most people I know, and there is always a fear of making things too complex. But I also have the tenacity to dig into information to check its voracity. I would hate to make a decision based on wrong information, which can cause mistakes, and ultimately can cause the loss of jobs.

Earlier I advised that we ran a DLO on a quarter percent margin, and there were no large 'just in case funds' as part of the process. We did a base budget exercise every year, with an extremely detailed set of 17 spreadsheets, with work profiled to the amount of working days a month.

Where an initiative would be self funding within the year, we would invariably go ahead with it. If something was going to save costs, we did it, but it had to save costs over the long term. We were a strongly environmentalist management team, but also worked strongly on the economy, so we approached recycling on a cost benefit basis, seeking the maximum benefit from the funds available.

The ability to make quick, timely decisions within service delivery situations is based upon a variety of circumstances, being certain of your data; in all areas is certainly one of the keys for me.

We had what we all agreed to be an Holistic awareness of the business, aware that if x happened over there, that y must happen somewhere else. Our accountant was promoted and inherited a less

than enviable task. To get the accounts meaningful, and satisfy some very demanding managers that wanted the right information at the right time.

We all used this as a development and learning exercise. He would prepare a draft set of accounts, we would highlight a few areas that looked questionable, and he would re-check those areas... these reiterations enabled progress towards the later 1/4 % margin capability.

He was always fascinated that I could ring about seven figure on ten pages in say five minutes, and that most of them would have an error. It was because I was immersed in the business that I instinctively knew that those finances couldn't align with the activities. He gradually learned these aspects of cause and effect, and these anomalies gradually faded away.

The most important aspect of all this was that people had the right information, at the right time to make the right decisions. You can not manage a high performance service based on infrequent information. Let me try an analogy:

I live in the Country now, and drive past miles of fields most days, at the edge of those fields are hedges, or at least for a couple of months a year, they are hedges. Compare your management of performance to a hedge! Humour me, its near the end of the book!

What sort of hedge do you want?

1. One that keeps your animals in, and visitors out?

2. One that shows you take a pride in your farm?

3. One that shows that you are an artist, and know how to create a fence out of living shrubs?

4. It's the edge of the garden, and it doesn't matter how far over the path it grows?

5. It's the edge of the garden, and I care for my property, and the community?

6. This is a very formal garden and the shaping of these hedges is crucial to it?

7. I've taken twenty years to create this swan, and it's getting better!

There is a real difference between the management style - planting birch twigs, and black poplars, and running round with a side arm flail once every six years, to the daily manicure that the swans need on top of the hedges above.

Performance management is not much different, to enable the very best performances you must have systems, and information that are managed in proportion to your required outcomes. It's equally important not to over manage, or stifle some areas. The farmers hedges are fit for purpose if they keep the animals in, and certain terrors out. So they don't need daily manicures.

I mentioned earlier that a housing association moved to 100% jobs on time for the first time ever, within three months of my arrival, what made that difference?

The main changes were to improve their input and use of the computer system, and get better reports on a daily basis for the manager in charge of allocating work. Having watched him work, and looked at the reports used most days, I asked whether he would use more information if it were given to him in a better format. He was pleased with the ideas so long as the technological impact was small, i.e that calling off the new reports was similar to the existing methods.

We created three reports which he could pull off daily, one showing him all emergency jobs that must be complete today, all urgent jobs needing to be complete by tomorrow, and the third being all routine jobs that had to be complete by next week.

This replaced and, or complimented existing reports, giving the possibility to deal with the immediate work, and gave a little more time to sort out the larger jobs. Both emergency and urgent jobs immediately went to 100% on time from the day that he had the reports, and routine joined them at 100% the next month.

I followed up with an investigation of what caused emergency jobs to go out of time, and found two causes. The main reason was because the computer completions process defaulted to the Sunday of the week the work was issued which had to be over-written when completing the work on the computer, and secondly that work that would take at least three working days to complete was put out as an emergency (to be completed in one day). There had only been ten reported overdue emergency jobs from April to November, one of those was genuinely late by the BVPI definitions, the other nine were on time!

The former was cured by putting on a visual / audible flag in the computer if a job was being entered as overdue, to ensure valid data was being entered, the second started with a gradual re-education of staff entering the urgency of coding in the first place.

The performance manager was shown the inaccuracy of her reports, both in that data didn't correspond to itself, and that most failures were not actually failures at all. She was more concerned that the auditor shouldn't be aware of the long term over reporting of a worse performance than was reality, than that they had been deluding themselves with mediocrity when they were actually very much UQ.

The next most important part of Performance management is to understand the specification you are supposedly monitoring and managing. The array of BVPI's from the Audit Commission is considerable for local government alone, without looking at health and the emergency services.

One BVPI has a 65 page manual to show how to do it, with masses of details of how and when to measure what, and then mandates for what frameworks these fit in for sending to the all powerful auditors. I was very pleased to get an instruction for my DC to fudge the results, as the one size fits all, didn't fit!

In general, definitions are usually quite well defined, which after all is appropriate. Yet there are still many authorities with conflicting instructions, due to auditor variation. One council that I was working for had had part of one BVPI 'Qualified', which meant they weren't monitoring it adequately. This in turn affected several linked BVPI's. This had a devastating affect of giving the worst possible score for that BVPI and several linked BVPI's.

Having dealt with these BVPI's in several Authorities, and 'done battle' for years on these with the Audit Commission and Defra about unrelated incorrect advice on the specification, I was fairly certain of my ground.

I spoke with their external auditor who had a finance background, and no knowledge of the area of operation. There was no budging her. I pointed out that I knew of no other authority in the Country that had a similar qualification, even though they worked the same way.

The council needed to get out of jail on this, so I devised some statistically relevant trials to sample and prove data, made a very academic presentation of results, in a style that was 'auditor' through and through. The exercise cost £3,000 to run, and would have to run every six months at about £2,500 a time there-after. This got the approval for the BVPI's, and proved that they were right all the time!

This very much goes back to the way I used to captain my Rugby Team, "know the laws of the game, and play to the referee." There is little point arguing with the man with the whistle, in rugby you go back ten metres if you argue, in BV you simply doff your cap!

The messages for Performance management?

• Know the rules of the game
• Have good, up to date information regularly
• Manage with that information
• Keep the processes appropriate to the needs and specifications.
• Have everyone involved in the process being managed, including front line forces (even when they are contractors, no, particularly if they are contractors)

- Ensure that the reporting is correct, ensuring you monitor the causes of failures, and deal with them
- Be sure you know where these BVPI's may be in the future.
- Don't assume your systems are sound, check their voracity in detail
- Use Challenge Partners to prevent complacency
- Thoroughly benchmark all services at least once every three years

I have criticised doing performance management from the centre, but not shown ways to ensure it occurs from the centres of activity. If an organisation can be passionate about service delivery, then, much the way that Tom Peters observed that; if you hang around a subject long enough, it will happen.

The ideal for me is that performance management needs to be driven from the centre, with the chief executive making it perfectly clear that every part of the organisation is to work to the corporate objectives of Continuous Improvement. There will be involvement, training, and constancy of purpose, and an open environment to question and probe at work done.

The need to explain common cause variation will disappear, and step improvements through system changes will be celebrated.

Effectively the organisation will carry out every aspect of PM with gusto, enabling all BVPI's to be fully dealt with all the time. A central team could deal with co-ordination of results, and help with the long term training of all people in the systems. That team could also support their customers with reviews, particularly where the 80/20 evaluation has promoted that area to the fore.

There would be: Joy at work, people would be pleased to attend, there would be less stress, more involvement and far less blame for mistakes. Where there is an internal Challenge, the views should be listened to, learned from corrected if not right, and acted on if needed. Thus a defensive attitude would also reduce. Staff turnover is likely to reduce as a result.

If that all sounds too far fetched, I have achieved most of it, even within a wider C&C, MBD environment, and spoken to others that

work in a business / service where that is truly the way the business works.

Some forms of half – way house is possible, and will occur as the organisation develops. There needs to be an open mind on this, and then a vision / commitment to see it through, not just as another initiative, but as a long term strategy at the corporate heart.

CHAPTER NINE:

Getting Started

A book like this loses value if some form of starting point is not given. Where you would want to start will vary with your background and perceived needs.

While presenting a recent seminar on operational matters, I asked: "How many of you are routinely involved in change management?" Virtually everyone put their hands up. I asked, "How many would expect the level of performance to go down while changing a service?" There were a few less hands up. I then asked, "How many of you have been formally trained in managing change?" There weren't many hands up then!

Managing change is one of those aspects that will make or break an organisation, and those people within it. If your aspiration is limited to making a 2.5% efficiency gain per annum, you may be able to do this without assistance, although in the latter years it will become more of an issue. If your aspirations must be greater than that, then something else is needed.

The Deming forum meets once a year, and could be a little overwhelming for someone on day one of their possible new approach to continuous improvement. That is virtually how I started, and have thanked the day I decided to register.

The books listed in the next chapter will help; again don't start with Freedom from Command and Control'unless you can deal with high level thinking in new areas quickly.

A change of this magnitude will be about your style and ambitions. How do you like to get to a position of making decisions? Perhaps start with reading one or two of the Deming pamphlets, for a single book try Out of the Crisis, perhaps go to a seminar, or speak with a change manager specialising in continuous improvement.

The internet with powerful search engines gives lots of options. Certainly searching on Deming alone would keep you busy for a long while.

If you are planning to use an interim manager or consultant, seek someone who communicates well, not only with you, but with your team. Seek empathy. Have they been involved with similar services to you? Do they understand the breadth of service requirements, BVPI's and legislation? Does that matter?

If you are into surfing the web, check out their case histories. Are they relevant to you and your work? Are the performances and changes they have implemented significant? i.e is there a really inspiring set of outcomes, or so little information that you are not convinced that a change for the better is inevitable or even ever occurred for them?

Some web-sites allude to a great deal, but give nothing for free. If an organisation is so concerned about secrecy that they will not openly share all the best with you, and enable you to become a learning organisation. Will they be good at enabling you to not need consultants to do the second, third and forth phases of change?

Consider style: If you are a person of few words, then I'm surprised you got this far with this book, but you certainly will not like my website! If you are a person that needs to see detail to believe, are the case histories just too thin and bland? Seek comfort, with a good fit between what you are and where this person may take you. Try a simple way forward from here using the tools that are provided throughout this book.

1. Use the PDCA cycle

a. Plan what you would want from an intervention

b. Do some research, what is available and might be possible?

c. Check who and what is around, how well they can help you, and how important you and your project are to them?

d. Act on this now.

2. Collate what information you have, and how well that compares to neighbours and best in class. What would you aspire to achieve? What must be achieved? Which areas are most important? Do you need to create savings as a result of this.

3. Try to format this in a cause and effect chart, perhaps with BVPIs, teams to address, constraining aspects, simply identify what you know, and perhaps identify areas where there are things that you don't know.

4. Test these ideas out with your team, your boss or someone as a sounding board, get authority if it is needed.

5. What in your wildest dreams would success look like? Write it down, how much time and effort would that be worth to achieve?

6. Start an intervention, with a guaranteed level of support by you and your team. The sooner you start, the greater the potential for success exceeding your dreams!

7. Whatever you do, don't do nothing!

Acknowledgements and suggested further reading

This is a real position of where to start and where to finish!

There are so many important people and organisations to mention, that it is probably safer to keep it short rather than go into an Oscars style list down to best boy, whatever one of those is.

My personal transformation to a change manager would never have got there without W. Edwards Deming and the Deming Forum, with particular references to Hazel Cannon, Professor Henry Neave and Ian Graham who helped me get started.

My later mentors have been John Seddon and Ian Fleming (not of 007 fame).

There have been some exceptional managers who have helped me on the road to management.The first to spend time supporting me rather than tolerate less than acceptable work was Bob Houghton. It's always worth remembering people who genuinely add value.

I can not understate the value of my relationship with PSnet, their network of contacts, and ability to cross support one another is brilliant. They also have the best value for money benchmarking systems I have found in the country.

As to reading and contacts:

There are about 26 booklets from the Deming Forum they are easy to read, and will help create new questions. In addition I would recommend:

Out of the Crisis	W Edwards Deming
The New Economics	W Edwards Deming
Freedom from Command & Control	John Seddon
The Case against ISO 9000	John Seddon
I want you to cheat	John Seddon
The Team Handbook	Peter Scholtes
The Leaders Handbook	Peter Scholtes
Harnessing the ParaBrain	Tony Buzan

Abbreviations and terminology used:

Act	Act of Parliament
Assisted (collection) person(s)	Refuse collection for infirm or disabled
BC	Borough Council
Blue Collar	Previous terminology for non-professional workforce
BV	Best Value
BVPI	Best Value Performance Indicator
C&C	Command and Control
CBT	Cross Boundary Tendering (one Council trying to work for another)
CC	Call Centre (Place where people handle customer calls, complaints etc.)
CCT	Compulsory Competitive Tendering
CI	Continuous Improvement
Client	Officers representing the Council on behalf of Customers

CPA	Comprehensive Performance Assessment (MoT test for a public body)
CSP	Cleaner Safer Places (Specific BV Review for a LB)
CRM	Customer Relationship Management (IT system to log work requests, etc.)
DC	District Council
DLO	Direct Labour Organisation (Workforce under the LGPLA 1980)
DSO	Direct Service Organisation (Workforce under 1988 LGA)
Fishbone Analysis	System to order data quickly for easy recognition (Cause & Effect)
Flow Chart	Simple way to show the order of work, including decision making process.
Gershon	Government advisor, report now requires annual 2.5% efficiency gain
HA	Housing Association
H&S	Health and Safety
HoS	Head of Service
IiP	Investors in People
ISO 9001	Quality Assurance system (9001, 2 or 3 at the time)
ISO 14001	Environmental Management standard
IT	Information Technology
JD	Job Description
KPI	Key Performance Indicator
LA	Local Authority
LG	Local Government
LGA 1988	Local Government Act 1988 (expanded CCT quite widely)
LGPLA 1980	Local Government Planning and Land Act (forced CCT for 1st time)

MBD	Management by Distrust (Systems set based on worst employees)
O&M (study)	Organisational and Management study to assess time for a job)
Pareto Analysis	Weighting of data – usually with an 80/20 rule.
PDCA	Plan Do Check Act
PI's	Performance Indicators
PMgt	Performance Management
PSnet	Public Sector Network (Support organisation to network services)
Remedies	Correction action after doing work incorrectly
RM	Response Maintenance (series of usually minor Housing Repairs)
Run Chart	Data presentation to show long term performances
SLA	Service Level Agreement (Pseudo internal contract)
SoR	Schedule of Rates (RM jobs described to a specification)
SWOT	Strengths, Weaknesses, Opportunities and Strengths. (Ability evaluation)
TQM	Total Quality Management
TUPE	Transfer of Undertakings, Protection of Employment regulations
UQ	Upper Quartile (being in the best 25% in the Country)
VfM	Value for Money

**This is the end of the first half of the book - Quality of Politics.
To read the second half - Politics or Quality, turn the book over.**

The Japanese call it Kaizen – the state when all the people in an organisation are working to improve the way in works.

In the UK, Continuous Improvement and Best Value have become the Holy Grail for 21st century public service providers.

But against a background of interference from central government and apathy from the electorate how do today's local authority managers drive forward the quality agenda in their organisations?

There is no single easy answer to fit all – but there is an approach which offers a way to address how their organisation actually works.

Dave Gaster draws on his years of experience as a senior local authority manager and consultant to offer colleagues a way forward in this quest for quality.

Drawing on examples from housing maintenance, refuse collection and other front line public services Quality or Politics focuses on how best to achive real quality and some of the characteristics which make quality easier to achieve.